Critical Thinking in Health and Social Care

Stella Jones-Devitt and Liz Smith

SAGE Publications
Los Angeles ▪ London ▪ New Delhi ▪ Singapore

SAGE Publications Ltd
1 Oliver's Yard
55 City Road
London EC1Y 1SP

SAGE Publications Inc.
2455 Teller Road
Thousand Oaks, California 91320

SAGE Publications India Pvt Ltd
B 1/I 1 Mohan Cooperative Industrial Area
Mathura Road
New Delhi 110 044

SAGE Publications Asia-Pacific Pte Ltd
33 Pekin Street #02-01
Far East Square
Singapore 048763

Library of Congress Control Number: 2006939788

British Library Cataloguing in Publication data

A catalogue record for this book is available from
the British Library

ISBN 978–1–4129–2069–8
ISBN 978–1–4129–2070–4 (pbk)

Typeset by Newgen Imaging Systems (P) Ltd, Chennai, India
Printed in India at Replika Press Pvt. Ltd
Printed on paper from sustainable resources

To Tre, Dave and Grace

Stella Jones-Devitt

To my parents Alan and Dorothy

Liz Smith

CONTENTS

FOREWORD

Critical thinking: some observations

Arguably, today's health and social care professionals – be they student aspirants or experienced practitioners – can be characterised as context-rich and time-poor. Why then might they wish to 'think about critical thinking'? Is there a case to be made? Jones-Devitt and Smith demonstrate powerfully the ways in which the idea of 'the professional' can be deconstructed and reformed through critical thinking; how context can be explored, challenged, explained and understood by means of a channelled scepticism; and how time and tasks might be better aligned where traditional ways-of-doing are subject to reflective and systematic scrutiny.

In a world where significant human endeavour (and ideology) turns on the quest for certainty and assertions of truth, the authors encourage the reader not simply to re-focus on the question itself; but also, more profoundly, they require us to question the question. Thereby, they take issue with what might be labelled, beyond postmodernism, as the 'cult of certainty'.

Through exposure to a well-articulated (but not unnecessarily burdensome) array of perspectives and tools, we are lured into new approaches to intellectual enquiry and innovation that will render such key activities as clinical decision-making or the design of care packages more robustly defensible in the changing context(s) of modern health and social care practice.

Importantly, the authors develop simple pedagogical devices to prevent any artificial divide or hierarchical separation of theories and practice. Questions, issues and dilemmas permeate the text. They are directed at our everyday professional experiences in ways which engage and provoke response(s). This culminates, beyond some well-articulated case-study material, in a compelling set of claims that only by acquiring the skills to recognise and address critical uncertainties, drawing on the repertoire of critical thinking approaches, will we be equipped to influence future policy and practice for improved health and social care services.

Accordingly, I believe the book will serve well a diverse audience – in policy formulation and practice determination at all levels – who are committed to the nation's health and well-being.

Dianne Willcocks, 28 February 2007

PREFACE

This book aims to explore key concepts of critical thinking and it considers their application to health and social care practice. The book helps the reader to examine the nature and relevance of critical thinking per se; it also seeks to familiarise the reader with a number of critical perspectives which can then be used to examine contemporary issues in health and social care. To contextualise the learning, workplace exercises and theoretical scenarios are suggested, in order to engage the reader in considering any implications for their own professional practice and operational effectiveness.

So why is this book needed and why now? We drew upon our own sense of 'muddling through' and considered the critical uncertainties bound up in health and social care in the present day. We perceive that the pace of change and fragmentation has escalated across both sectors: throughout this book we allude to the prevailing perceptions of the emergent knowledge economy, based upon key neoliberal suppositions of flexibility, accountability and active consumerism; the growth of this economy appears to have gathered an irresistible momentum, spawning new types of 'professional' worker roles that are developing across many occupational sectors. This book seeks to help the practitioner make sense of this pace and fragmentation through developing an understanding and awareness of the wider ideological drivers for policy provision and change, whilst providing some tools that can help to reconnect and locate everyday practice in the emerging context.

At the time of writing this book, we found little published material concerned with enabling health and social care practitioners at strategic/consultant level to conduct critical examination of their own practice, alongside applying some newer ways of thinking to specific contexts: we hope that this book begins to occupy that space.

Given the shifting contexts and blurring of boundaries between health and social care domains, we have taken some liberties with the word 'professional' within this text: the term is used euphemistically to imply a professional approach via an implicit set of values, responsibilities and strategic obligations that being 'professional' involves. It is not our intention to delineate between the qualified and non-qualified; hence, we recognise that career development, professional roles and nomenclature are not only linked to profession-specific occupations in either domain. We also found that certain areas within health and social care are difficult to segregate as belonging wholly to one or other faction; thus within the book, public health examples are used to illustrate this shared agenda.

The book is divided into three discrete sections. Section 1, 'A Theoretical Overview' provides an insight into how critical thinking skills knowledge is constructed, privileged and applied, covering: some of the key debates about definitions and use of critical thinking; the authenticity of knowledge and resonance for the contemporary social infrastructure; how assumptions effect thinking and influence professional stereotyping; alongside the nature of 'evidence' in which specific paradigms are presented, contrasted and debated.

In Section 2, 'Key Theoretical Tools of Critical Thinking', we examine some of the conceptual tools available for sense making in the domain and consider the possible implications for practice. Where appropriate, chapters in this section examine theoretical similarities and differences amongst selected theories and assess their relationship to strategic application. All the conceptual tools are selected according to their relevance to current health and social care policy-making and practice. Five theoretical critiques were chosen by the contributing authors, but many more could have been selected. Given the plethora of potential tools, readers are encouraged to apply any theoretical tool of their own personal choosing, as they see fit for their own context.

In Section 3, 'Application to Health and Social Care Practice', several case studies and scenarios are explored through the application of critical thinking skills, allowing the reader to actively apply the learning to the workplace and examine the implications and further resonance.

It is worth noting that this book is about 'applied' critical thinking skills within the health and social care domain. Given these parameters, we decided to exclude mathematical notions of reasoning and exercises in numerical analysis, psychological theories of thought processing and developmental learning alongside 'heavy' philosophical theorising about the nature of thinking per se. Ideally, we are hopeful that the book provides the health and social care strategist with an array of tools that can be applied to first order practice; it is not aiming to be a comprehensive tome about critical thinking in all its forms, nor to fulfil any kind of purist academic agenda. We encountered some difficulties when trying to tease out the precise boundaries for health and social care respectively; consequently, fluid contemporary interpretations of both aspects have led us to assume a 'blurred boundary' position in the book on many occasions.

Each chapter contains specific pedagogical features that comprise a concise introduction, learning objectives, an end-of-chapter summary, case studies (where appropriate), specific problem-solving scenarios, additional workplace exercises, and sources of further reading and exploration. The latter provide detail of specific print and web-based resources in critical thinking skills development, and are complementary to the exercises in the text.

To use this book most productively, we suggest that all readers familiarise themselves with Section 1, which gives a good grounding in essential critical thinking debates, principles and concepts. Once completed, the reader can then selectively discern the most appropriate tools from Section 2 to apply to their own workplace context. Section 3 then acts as an aide-memoir of critical thinking skills analysis, in relation to some contemporary health and social care issues.

We have enjoyed putting this book together for health and social care practitioners and our sincerest thanks go to all those who have contributed both directly and indirectly to its production. Specific thanks go to Peter Draper and Julie Dickinson for their well considered contributions to several chapters in this text. During the process, we have also extended our own knowledge and enthusiasm for using critical thinking approaches within health and social care, and trust that this book does the same for its readers.

Stella Jones-Devitt and Liz Smith

LIST OF ILLUSTRATIONS

Figures

Tables

Section 1

A THEORETICAL OVERVIEW

1

THINKING CRITICALLY ABOUT CRITICAL THINKING

Stella Jones-Devitt and Liz Smith

This chapter explores some of the contrasting definitions of critical thinking. It considers the background, development and possible boundaries of critical thinking as a subject area. It also raises questions about the purpose and politics of critical thinking studies taught in higher education. Exercises are included to facilitate your personal construction of the characteristics of critical thinking.

Chapter aim

- To provide an overview of some key debates about critical thinking

Learning outcomes

After studying this chapter, you should be able to:

- explore the background and development of critical thinking
- critically discuss some of the contrasting definitions of critical thinking
- identify possible boundaries of critical thinking as a discrete subject area and body of knowledge
- critically evaluate the purpose and politics of contemporary 'Critical Thinking Studies'

Background and development

Critical thinking is often linked with a multitude of synonyms such as 'creative thinking', 'lateral thinking', 'problem-solving', 'decision-making' and 'reasoning'. Given these different descriptors, origins of critical thinking are also contested, ranging from those who trace it back to the times of Socrates and the Ancient Greeks in which assumptions that those in 'authority' had sound knowledge and insight were challenged, to those who view critical thinking as a fundamentally modern construct. This latter perspective is held by Boychuk Duchscher (1999) who contends that critical thinking evolved from the efforts of the early twentieth-century Frankfurt School of Critical Social Theory. This School of thinking emerged in response to the unsuccessful integration of capitalism and socialism in Eastern Europe which raised much dissent about the lived experience of everyday lives and the relationship to belief systems; out of which came the Critical Social Theorists' views about critiquing ideology as a form of social oppression rather than accepting it as an all pervading force.

Daly (1998) draws attention to the Middle Ages and the teachings of Thomas Aquinas who systematically explored each part of any idea with rigorous scrutiny before letting his thoughts develop further. Renaissance thinkers also began to think that human life should be subject to more examination, especially in those areas concerned with religious matters, art, nature and freedom. Between the fifteenth and seventeenth centuries several scholars emerged such as Francis Bacon and Thomas More in England. Bacon is credited with writing the first book concerned explicitly with critical thinking entitled 'The Advancement of Learning' (1605) in which he described several 'false idols' that impinge upon peoples' ability to think if left to their own devices. Many of these idols helped to form incorrect assumptions, especially in relation to misuse of words, blind acceptance of convention, self-delusion and poor instruction. Thomas More's notion of 'Utopia' (1516) envisaged a society without private property that he advocated as an idyll. Heywood (2004) suggests that More's work could be viewed as satirical rather than propagandist. Heywood also indicates that such notions of utopian society emerged at this time due to faith in reason that encouraged: 'thinkers to view human history in terms of progress, but it also, perhaps for the first time, allowed them to think of human and social development in terms of unbounded possibilities' (p. 365).

Within this historical period of Enlightenment, also known as the Age of Reason, philosophers and political thinkers eschewed religious dogma and metaphysical forces as the key drivers for existence, instead basing their ideas upon human rationalism and reason. Considerable activity revolved around French thinkers like Descartes, Diderot and Rousseau who focussed on rationalist explanations in which they argued that the workings of the physical and social worlds could be understood by an examination of reason alone. Descartes is credited with writing the second explicitly stated book of critical thinking 'Rules for the Direction of the Mind' (1628) in which the need for a systematic set of principles to guide the mind and thinking processes were espoused. From this work, Descartes went on to explore possible dichotomies of mind and body, with the mind being defined as a thinking machine separate of physical functioning. Descartes proposed that both should be treated as independent systems rather than as one, thus spawning an approach known as Cartesian Dualism upon which much of modern medicine is predicated. These views contributed to an examination of existing political orders and underpinned many radical and revolutionary doctrines. Heywood (2004) notes that key thinkers began to appreciate the potential of human beings for self-determination or to: 'the extent that human beings possess the capacity to understand their world, they have the ability also to improve or reform it' (p. 21).

Europe in the seventeenth and eighteenth centuries was a time of great challenge to existing social orders and hierarchies. From Hobbes and Locke in England, to Machiavelli in Italy, to Voltaire in France; all recognised that disciplined human minds were well-placed to question the real agendas of the establishment in political power and submit those in privilege and authority to real scrutiny and accountability. Given the context of these times, it is hardly surprising to find that both the American Revolution (1776) and French Revolution (1789) occurred during this period, in which those in privilege and power faced brutal scrutiny and questioning of their actions. The rationale underpinning these events were explored in the American Thomas Paine's seminal work, 'The Rights of Man' (1791) in which the justification for both revolutions was made as being actions undertaken by conscious and critical efforts to remove inequalities fostered by the privileging of heredity and monarchy. Throughout the revolutionary period and subsequent aftermath, the power of collective critical thought became recognised as an enduring force for meaningful political change. This spawned a new direction in which critical thinking and reason were applied as tools for specific domains in the pre-industrialised world; examples include Adam Smith's economic treatise 'The Wealth of Nations' (1776) and Immanuel Kant's application to reason, per se, in his 'Critique of Pure Reason' (1781).

The nineteenth-century industrial era saw critical thinking being applied directly to prevailing economic issues with both Marx and Engels using reasoning tools to critique the emergence and possible consequences of the capitalist state and to scrutinise the power of manipulated thought. A central tenet of Marx's analysis was the explanation of the status quo and the relationship to class consciousness. Marx and Engels alluded to notions of 'False Consciousness' in which a dominant ideology or set of ideas, propounded by the ruling class, become so powerful that the dominated class fails to recognise their own exploitation and consequently remained uncritical and unaware of any power to resist or challenge. The emergence of a range of social sciences, grounded in reason, yet removed from the deductive logic dominating the physical sciences, added further weight to the growing use of critical thinking to unpack the processes of both knowledge construction and its privileging; also being applied to the unconscious mind through the work of Sigmund Freud and other psychoanalysts.

In the early twentieth century, the educationalist John Dewey added a further dimension to the development of critical thinking, suggesting that it could be linked to higher-order sense making in a world where ambiguity caused dilemmas that required consideration of alternatives. Dewey indicated that critical thinking was one element of a broader reflective framework involving assessment, scrutiny and conclusion; a process that should be followed if effective judgements were to be made. According to Daly (1998) Dewey felt that the main purpose of critical thinking was to introduce an appropriate degree of scepticism and rigour alongside suspension of judgement when necessary. McKendree et al. (2002) add that Dewey saw critical thinking as an essential tool for the furtherance of viable and meaningful democracies. This approach also aligns him with the Critical Social Theorists of the early twentieth century mentioned previously, who saw ideological critique as central to understanding routes of social oppression.

Clearly the contributions of certain historical figures have aided the overall development of critical thinking, yet many groups are not represented at all in traditional historical analyses. Difficulties arise when trying to deduce who has been left out of the historical documentation and why. A pattern for inclusion is prevalent in respect of the characteristics of the key critical thinkers presented, in that they were: men, of privileged social background, predominantly white and well-educated.

Activity

- In your opinion, who is the most well-known critical thinker in contemporary times?
- Why is there a dearth of women critical thinkers in history?
- Identify someone from your own professional area who is a critical thinker

---

Definitions of critical thinking

Given this historical predominance of men from privileged backgrounds within critical thinking, it still appears to be dominated by similar theorists in contemporary times. Many commentators have sought to provide a definitive view of critical thinking yet there is no overall consensus of opinion; merely a collection of responses that can be clustered into several domains. Table 1.1 provides some of the many contrasting definitions of critical thinking to consider.

Even these five examples show considerable differences between two continua. The first continuum concerns whether critical thinking is an instrumental or non-instrumental activity. Certain theorists see critical thinking as a highly instrumental activity in which outcomes are linked to discernible goals and targets. Halpern (1989) in particular, defines critical thinking as being goal-driven in essence, whereas Paul (1995) sees it as an abstract non-instrumental activity to defend. The other continuum in which opinion is polarised,

Table 1.1 Definitions of critical thinking

Definition	Source	Comments
An approach to ideas from the standpoint of deliberate consideration	Harris (2001)	Involves notion of 'distancing' in order to be dispassionate and thus arriving at a more effective judgement
Reasonable, reflective thinking that is focused on what to believe and do	Ennis (1995)	Implies that an 'active' dimension should be present; process underpinned by an instinctive quality linked to beliefs
Thinking about your thinking, while you're thinking, to make it better, more clear, accurate and defensible	Paul (1995)	Primarily abstract activity that enables a robust defence
Thinking that is purposeful, reasoned and goal directed	Halpern (1989)	Highly instrumental process that is target-driven in essence
The ability to solve problems by making sense of information using creative, intuitive, logical and analytical mental processes . . . and the process is continual	Snyder (1993)	Seeks answers using a range of potentially conflicting attributes

concerns whether thinking has to have an 'active' dimension or end-point. Harris (2001) implies that thinking is about the process of distancing from specific standpoints in order to arrive at the best possible accommodation which may, or may not, involve acting out one's thoughts. In this definition, the whole process is underpinned by reflective thinking. This contrasts with Ennis' (1985) assertions stating that thinking should lead to enactive processes.

These continua are mediated by whether the process of critical thinking is viewed essentially as engagement in problem-solving as opposed to sense-making per se. A problem-solving approach aligns with active and goal driven responses that are primarily time-limited and discreet activities, whilst sense-making can be an abstract and continuous process linked to the thinker rather than to specific tasks undertaken (see Figure 1.1).

After considering many contrasting views, the broad definition of critical thinking that underpins the ethos of this book comprises:

> Making sense of the world through a process of questioning the questions, challenging assumptions, recognising that bodies of knowledge can be chaotic and evolving; ultimately with the aim of continually improving thinking.

Activity

- Which of the above definitions is the most appealing?
- Do you always act out your thinking?
- Are you primarily a problem solver or sense-maker?

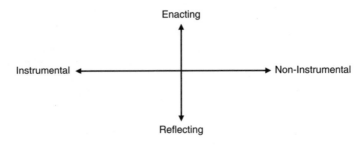

Figure 1.1   Critical thinking continua

Possible boundaries of critical thinking

In order to explore possible boundaries for critical thinking, it is also important to consider the current social context for both positioning and curriculum. McKendree et al. (2002) note that an interest in critical thinking has accelerated since the early 1980s. They ascribe this to the changing nature of both social and economic infrastructures in which: 'Turn-of-the Millennium life-styles, including the information overload that accompanies the growth of electronic networks, mean that being able to think critically is essential to be able to respond appropriately to rapid and complex changes in modern society' (p. 58).

Flexibility is clearly the new byword for modern times: in economic terms, individuals and organisations have to show they are responsive to change in order to survive. They need to be able to foster reinvention of self and purpose in a fast-moving economic climate. It is in this complex and often chaotic context that critical thinking has re-emerged. However, the sort of critical thinking that has been given priority mirrors the need for quick-fix solutions and problem-solving. Curricula are now aligned to technical-rationalist and instrumental approaches. Barnett (1997) calls this the rise of 'New Technicism' in which different stakeholders wield varying amounts of power and influence over curricular matters that were previously none of their business (e.g. economic development agencies and funding councils). He asserts that this ascendancy has led to: a move towards competency rather than understanding; superficial skills acquisition rather than deeper and more specific forms of development; a focus on individual rather than collective performance. This is a somewhat ironic shift given the broad conceptualisation of critical thinking as an enduring lifelong enterprise, described by Facione and Facione (1996) as: 'a habit of mind, a part of one's character' (p. 129).

Models for teaching critical thinking fall into three broad areas:

- as a pure subject per se
- completely embedded within another subject or vocational area

- a mixed approach, in which critical thinking can be applied and embedded, yet recognised and studied as a discreet subject

McKendree et al. (2002) suggest that the mixed approach may reap most benefits as this: 'provides opportunities for practice in a variety of contexts and at the same time reinforces those skills taught in subjects' (p. 58). The mixed and the totally embedded models appear to be most popular approaches at present. These allow vocational areas such as nursing and teaching to apply critical thinking principles to their policy and practice. Boychuk Duchscher (1999) implies that the emergence of critical thinking in nursing comes from the need to address social, economic and international health challenges. In North American nurse training programmes, critical thinking has become one of the established pre-requisites for nurse education and the Canadian Nurses Association is also committed to exploring critical thinking as an essential nursing construct.

McKendree et al. (2002) note that critical thinking skills are now given increasing priority by educational policy makers, reflecting a growing belief in: 'the importance of learners' developing thinking skills, not only as a tool with which to maximise potential in individual subjects but also as a generic skill to be learned in classes and transferred from one to another' (p. 57). This focus is unsurprising, especially as the practical use of such skills helps meet the philosophical shift towards instrumentalism and output orientation expected of a 'knowledge-production' society.

Boychuk Duchscher (1999) contends that the possible content base of any critical thinking curriculum should comprise: Meta-cognition – in which thinking about the 'quality' of thinking is considered; dialectical reasoning – in which two or more opposing views compete; reflection – in which the consequences of actions and activities are explored. However, the dialectical reasoning element is contested by several theorists. Harris (2001) asserts that dialectical notions are often misinterpreted as thinking that has an 'either/or' dichotomy. Harris adds that it is often the ability to 'ungeneralise' rather than polarise that enhances critical thinking and sense-making skills. McKendree et al. (2002) also note that either/or dichotomies can lead to over-emphasising the problem-solving dimensions of critical thinking. They believe that 'problem-finding' rather than problem-solving is often more valuable, especially in areas where conflicts may be irresolvable when only focused upon one specific facet, stating that: 'students need to understand that such "questioning the question" is sometimes a very good thing to do' (p. 64).

Brookfield (1987) adds to the debate about curricular content with a schema that has four elements: identifying and challenging assumptions – in which assumptions are examined for accuracy and validity; the importance of context – in which, the wider context of people's lived experience is acknowledged as being central to their sense-making processes; exploring and imagining alternatives – in which critical thinkers continually try to uncover different ways of perceiving their world; reflective scepticism – in which the thinker is cautious about accepting new or universal truths and acknowledges the impact that new information or ideas can make upon their previous knowledge boundaries. Brookfield's (1987) process-based approach goes far beyond the quick-fix and primarily superficial problem-solving focus of populist critical thinking self-help guides that are gaining unfortunate precedence.

Although precise boundaries are impossible to dictate, there are some discernible commonalities across critical thinking curricula that are valuable for skills development and enhancement. These can be treated as discreet critical thinking elements, embedded within other subjects, or mixed to provide a strong theoretical base that enhances application to other contexts:

- Meta-cognition
  This should explore thinking about thinking but should also include an exploration of definitions, conceptualisations and possible boundaries of critical thinking.
- Knowledge
  This component needs to include an examination of the privileging of knowledge and explore the relationship between knowledge production and ownership.
- Assumptions
  Critical thinkers need to appraise assumptions in light of their validity and enduring nature. Notions of context and tensions between universal truths and multiple realities help define the key issues.
- Evidence
  Effective thinkers should be able to evaluate different forms of evidence. In order to do this, the curriculum should explore the parameters and tensions of so-called scientific and non-scientific forms of evidence.

Scenario

You are the Education, Training and Development Manager of a public service industry, employing around 2,500 people regionally. A new Chief Executive has been appointed recently and she is really committed to developing and enhancing the problem-solving skills of the whole workforce. Prior to joining your organisation, she attended a leadership and management short course in which problem-solving skills were discussed in one of the sessions on 'critical thinking'. She asks you to develop a half-day critical thinking skills training session for all employees that promotes problem-solving techniques in the workplace. She expects you to gain tangible short-term results from this initiative that impact upon both employees and workplace performance indicators.

(Continued)

Questions

- Do you agree to develop the sessions?
- What are the major problems with this approach?
- How does what you are being asked to do reconcile with you own conceptualisation of critical thinking?
- How would you take forward critical thinking skills development in your own organisation?

Purpose and politics of contemporary critical thinking 'studies'

As discussed by McKendree et al. (2002) there has been an upsurge in critical thinking as a discreet subject area since the 1980s. It is now commonplace to find critical thinking curricula in a variety of guises and levels from school-based learning to higher education and also integrated within organisational training and development programmes and mission statements. However, on further analysis, what is often purported to be 'critical thinking' is in reality: 'Too many facts, too little conceptualizing, too much memorizing and too little thinking' (Hurd, cited in Paul, 2004, p. 1). Paul (2004) describes three common facets that underpin critical thinking teaching in contemporary higher education:

1 Most higher education institutes do not have a cogent and substantive view of critical thinking.

This point is quite challenging, given that it is now de rigueur to have some reference to critical thinking in most university and faculty mission statements. Often this is addressed via enhancement of students' thinking and investigative skills rather than the institution showing a commitment to being a critical thinking organisation per se.

2 This lack is not acknowledged as institutions believe that, as higher education academics, they already understand critical thinking concepts and assume that they teach students adequately.

This lack of insight also relates to the first point about institutions assuming that only students need critical thinking skills enhancement. Many higher education institutes and academic staff conflate discursive analysis with higher-order thinking skills, using 'expertise' based upon density of a body of factual knowledge, as the singular measure of critical thinking authority.

3 Lectures, rote-learning/memorisation and short-term study habits are still the norm for teaching and learning in higher education.

There is awareness that deep learning takes place over time, utilising processes rather than outputs and the ability to make connections rather than in always providing answers. It is paradoxical that many of the learning and teaching methods employed in higher education do not offer adequate opportunities for such engagement, fostering superficial or 'surface' learning at best. Modularisation of subjects into discreet unique chunks of learning has not helped to develop an overall coherence in disciplinary areas. This chunking up of thinking has also led to the development of assessment grounded in reductive analyses reflecting this fragmentation of learning; hence, the proliferation of model answers, an increasing reliance on the testing of factual knowledge and the introduction of competency-based learning in higher education.

Activity

- What do you consider to be the difference between deep and surface learning?
- What type of learning predominates in your workplace?
- How do you 'know' what you know?

Paul (2004) suggests that critical thinking skills could be revolutionised in higher education if institutions started to teach content through thinking rather than content and then thinking. Exemplars include: history being taught as historical thinking, sociology as sociological thinking. He argues that with such an approach, the critical thinking curriculum is then used to:

foster the intellectual traits essential to critical thinking . . . to teach students to use critical thinking concepts as tools in entering into any system of thought, into any subject or discipline . . . to teach students to construct in their own minds the concepts that define the discipline . . . that enable students to master content using their thinking and to become skilled learners. (p. 5)

In relation to Paul's (2004) assertions about over-emphasising content, McKendree et al. (2002) also note that content-driven approaches lead to a paradox in teaching critical thinking skills known as 'Authoritative Democracy'. Given the need for critical thinking to inculcate thinking for one's self, the more directive a content-based curriculum becomes, then the less likely is the development of individual thinking skills. With such an approach there is often little slack if students wish to explore something in more depth than the explicit curriculum demands. This is compounded by forms of assessment which then actively reward the efforts of students who have followed the prescribed doctrinaire route in order to pass the assignment, whilst sacrificing thinking that challenges and usurps authoritative logic when appropriate.

A useful way to overcome narrow content-focused approaches is through the tactic of representation and context for thinking which McKendree et al. (2002) suggest is: 'about gaining the skills of fluency in building and transforming information in a personally meaningful way' (p. 59). They argue that without development of such skills, knowledge remains static and impenetrable. They state that:

> the best representation almost always lies beneath the surface of the given information and requires learners to engage in a deep way, often in collaboration with others, to impose their own framework on the problem. Further, representational systems are often very local to a particular problem or problem type and must be reinterpreted each time in the current context. (p. 59)

According to Brown and Duguid (1991) the act of making knowledge explicit means that it loses its power of impact; by 'boxing' critical thinking into a discrete and modularised subject, its effect is diluted and made safe. This has parallels with the Marxist perspective of false consciousness, as those who study critical thinking within the confines of Academia can be controlled and contained; it is much safer to allow playing out of some anarchistic thinking within the classroom than allowing it out onto the streets and into organisations.

Chapter summary

This chapter has explored some of the claims made for the historical antecedents of critical thinking. Its development has been linked far back to the ideas of the Ancient Greek philosophers, Socrates, Aristotle and Plato. Claims have been made for its emergence linked to Renaissance times and the Enlightenment period, in which 'natural order' and direct links with God, supernatural and metaphysical forces, were challenged for the first time as the sole drivers for existence. Critical thinking has also been constructed as a modern phenomenon that emerged out of a profound dissatisfaction with capitalism and ensuing market-force ideologies.

There is a plethora of definitions of critical thinking, ranging from notions of critical thinking as a highly structured and systematic way of solving problems through to viewing it as an intuitive and highly circumspect activity relating to generalised sense-making of the wider world. Two continua have been identified: instrumental to non-instrumental; enacting to reflective processes. What is clear is that there is still no overall consensus of the precise constituents of critical thinking, despite its gain in popularity as a subject studied closely over the last 25 years.

Possible boundaries of critical thinking are equally contested, with some theorists arguing that it has followed a technical-rationalist approach resulting in superficial application to problem-solving, that is without a deeper underpinning knowledge or establishment of the subject as a discipline per se. The proliferation of application in vocational contexts like nursing and teaching often reflects the use of critical thinking in its most instrumental guise: hence, its use as part of a technical toolkit in which most professional dilemmas can be both rationalised and solved. It is more useful to think about critical thinking as a process rather than as a set of outputs. Four common areas emerge during the 'process' of critical thinking, comprising: meta-cognition, which explores thinking about thinking; knowledge and its privileging; assumptions, which examine the relationship between universal truths and shifting realities; evidence, its nature and parameters.

This chapter finally considered the purpose and politics of teaching critical thinking in higher education contexts. Key points relate to: assumptions made by higher education institutes and academics that because of their very nature, they can make legitimate claims for critical thinking expertise; the modularisation and chunking up of learning and potential conflict with cultivating deep and coherent lifelong learning approaches in which critical thinking plays a substantial part. Politically, there is clear split between viewing critical thinking studies as a welcome part of the liberal, student-centred style of higher education that empowers and develops independence, contrasted by notions that critical thinking studies is really about anaesthetising dissent via the sanctity of the higher-education classroom.

Sources of further reading and exploration

Books

Cottrell, S. (2005) *Critical Thinking skills: Developing Effective Analysis and Argument.* Basingstoke: Palgrave Macmillan.

Ennis, R. H. (1995) *Critical Thinking.* Upper Saddle River, NJ: Prentice Hall.

Fisher, A. (2001) *Critical Thinking: An Introduction.* Cambridge: Cambridge University Press.

Halpern, D. (1996) *Thought and Knowledge: An Introduction to Critical Thinking* (3rd edition). Mahwah, NJ: Laurence Erlbaum Associates Inc.

Paul, R. and Elder, L. (2005) *Learn the Tools the Best Thinkers Use.* Upper Saddle River, NJ: Prentice Hall.

Web

The Critical Thinking Community: comprehensive US site covering resources, seminars, training and position papers. Available at: www.criticalthinking.org/

Critical Thinking on the Web: Tim van Gelder's unique repository of a range of subjects and insights related to critical thinking. Available at: www.austhink.org/critical/

2

THE AUTHENTICITY OF KNOWLEDGE

Stella Jones-Devitt and Liz Smith

This chapter considers the social construction and privileging of knowledge and the relationship to ideology. It examines the supposed growth and development of a 'Knowledge Industry' society alongside the global demise of manufacturing economies. It explores the implications of enforcing Service Industry workers to become knowledge producers per se. Some of the uncritical assumptions underpinning the reification of the knowledge industry are challenged; both in terms of its real existence and as a possible force for liberating individual workers from the oppression of material 'outputs'. For example, has there really been a shift in wealth creation from control of organisational and material resources to a dependence on individual 'expertise', and, hence, individual workers? Activities and exercises are included to assist in considering the relationship between knowledge, wider socio-economic issues and professional autonomy.

Chapter aim

- To consider the social construction and privileging of knowledge

Learning outcomes

After studying this chapter, you should be able to:

- examine the growth and development of a knowledge industry society in relation to wider notions of ideology
- critically appraise the transition from manufacturing economy to knowledge production economy
- explore the relationship between knowledge and professional autonomy

The development of a knowledge industry society

As noted in the previous chapter, one of the key areas involved in the process of critical thinking concerns knowledge and its privileging.

Knowledge per se is the essential raw material around which all critical thinking takes place. In order to understand how knowledge gains boundaries and value, it is important to link its development to concepts of ideology. According to Heywood (1998) the term 'ideology' (ideologie) was first used in public in 1796 by Antoine Destutt de Tracy during the French Revolution. As an avid Enlightenment thinker, de Tracy suggested that it referred to an emerging science of ideas which would eventually enjoy the same status as established sciences like physics and biology. Ideology, in this context, would play a keen role in determining the boundaries of acceptable knowledge.

Heywood (1998) suggests that ideology influences contemporary society in a number of ways: it provides an overarching framework through which the world is understood; it helps to set goals and inspires activity towards meeting these defined targets; ideology shapes political systems and governance; ideology provides what Gramsci (1935, cited in Heywood, 1998) defined as the 'commonsense' of the age, in which ideas and knowledge provide social and cultural cohesion and unification. Heywood (1998) also notes that the purpose of ideology, like critical thinking, is contested and has often been constructed historically in a pejorative manner. Marxist thinkers ascribe a very different meaning to ideology, linking the concept to notions of false consciousness and manipulated thought. Marx (1846, cited in Marx and Engels, 1976) described the notion in relation to the ruling elite as being about a process of delusion and mystification, in which the owners of material production inevitably hold control over all economic and social processes, including mental production and thinking.

Within the confines of the twentieth century, ideology became much more heavily linked with political dogma, corresponding with the rise of Fascism and Communism and a general intolerance of contrasting viewpoints. Heywood (1998) implies that it is only in recent history that ideology has returned to a relatively neutral apolitical position, being perceived of as: 'an action-oriented system of thought. So defined, ideologies are neither good nor bad, true nor false, open nor closed, liberating nor oppressive – they can be all these things' (p. 11). Regardless of whether ideology is viewed as intrinsically good or bad, it clearly provides a framework within which the search for knowledge occurs and highlights the depth at which ideological structures underpin knowledge acquisition and production.

If ideology can be defined as action-oriented and driven by instrumental concerns, it can be linked closely to the need for knowledge production required to match the demands of an ascendant economy, in which knowledge *is* the new industry. Edwards and Usher (2001) suggest that knowledge is being liberated from many conventions in order to supply the demands of a new information age. They note three key facets:

- Knowledge enjoys a new sense of unruliness in which the laws and conventions of natural sciences no longer bind
- Acceptance that knowledge has fluidity and changes over time via a process of diversification and contestation
- There is an enhanced awareness and knowledge of change processes which influence the relationship to acceptance, compliance and relevance of new knowledge production and its application at organisational levels

Curry (1997) contests some of the uncritical assumptions that underpin notions of living within an economic era in which knowledge and information have key significance in wealth creation. He questions the idea that the emerging 'knowledge worker' is the key protagonist in such wealth creation, indicating that the linear thinking that views the worker as owning the means of production (i.e. knowledge) is too simplistic. Blackler (1995) also notes the assumptions that perceive a shift in wealth creation from control of organisational and material resources to a dependence on individual 'expertise'. Curry (1997) challenges the ideas of Drucker (1993) which involve notions of a post-capitalist society in which he suggests that the knowledge worker is now at the centre of economic production due to the ideas held in their head. Curry (1997) indicates that unless knowledge and information have superseded manual labour as the key determinants of value then this is a flawed assumption, especially as social and economic relations are still mediated primarily by the exchange value of labour, albeit physical or mental. He describes this process as:

the material embodiment of dead, congealed, labour, and, by extension, information. A commodity is produced through the application of physical activity, knowledge and information. If, for a moment, we forget about capitalist commodities, capital, and value, and concentrate on information we can see that all material products of human activity contain, or embody information and/or knowledge. (p. 6)

Powell and Snellman (2004) suggest that the move into a knowledge industry is marked by an increase in intellectual capabilities rather than through a reliance on physical inputs and resources. Fenwick (2001) notes how this process increases corporate expectations placed upon workers rather than leading to increased autonomy as suggested in early knowledge industry literature. She describes how the contemporary workforce is expected to demonstrate effectiveness via the concept of the 'enterprising self' in which: 'individuals are expected to construct and self-regulate their own human capital in all spheres of life, subordinating their desires for development, meaning, fulfilment, relationships, even spirituality, to their work activity and work capacity' (p. 127).

Both Curry (1997) and Blackler (1995) suggest that there is a tendency to view knowledge in production as a concrete and somewhat reified entity, whereas it is more useful to analyse knowledge industry claims in terms of knowledge as a social 'process' running alongside more one-dimensional views of knowledge as a commodity. The precise constituents of a supposed knowledge industry or 'economy' are still contested; indeed Edwards and Usher (2001) lament the dearth of analysis in this area, indicating that knowledge production should be about who and for whom, as well as considering the what and how. Powell and Snellman (2004) describe how knowledge economy explanations and research approaches fall into three distinct areas as follows:

- The rise of new science-based industries
  This implies that the growth of technology and science-based industries, emerging from the 1960s onwards, has contributed to major social and economic change via innovations that have fuelled economic development and impacted upon everyday lifestyle choices.
- Knowledge intensive industries
  This is underpinned by the notion that particular niche industries have become leaders in knowledge production, resulting in productivity increases that have led to the emergence of new job roles and novel forms of work organisation that have wider socio-economic significance.
- Emergence of learning organisations
  This strand explores the place of learning and continuous innovation within organisations. It assesses why some companies appear to be particularly successful at knowledge production and transfer and the resonance for the wider market economy.

A further layer of complexity is added when assessing the characteristics of knowledge, per se. Curry (1997) defines two principal types of knowledge:

1 Imaginary or fantastical knowledge which is accepted as part of the historical knowledge base of society, yet has no direct relationship to material reality
2 Practical knowledge which is directly relevant to the material world.

The first definition refers to notions of self-enlightenment and metaphysical pondering in which wisdom, folklore and custom prevail, whilst the latter is technological, contemporary and applied directly to commodity production.

Blackler (1995) provides a further level of sophistication, indicating that knowledge can be sub-divided into five essential and often overlapping areas. His typology comprises the following:

- Embrained knowledge
  Dependent on conceptual skills and cognitive abilities, or 'knowledge about'.
- Embodied knowledge
  Primarily action oriented or explicit knowledge routed in specific contexts and practical thinking, also known as 'knowledge how'.

- Encultured knowledge
  Describes knowledge based upon shared understandings which are linked to socialisation and acculturation processes. This sort of knowledge is socially constructed and open to negotiation; it can be defined as 'contextualised knowledge'.
- Embedded knowledge
  Routine and systematic thinking related directly to institutional arrangements involving organisational frameworks and protocols, also described as 'organisational knowledge'.
- Encoded knowledge
  Involves information conveyed by signs or symbols which is then encoded and transmitted. This type of knowledge is highly selective and often decontextualised, also characterised as 'knowledge informating'.

Despite a lack of precision and a variety of contested theoretical claims, an overall understanding of knowledge has evolved over time from the Middle Ages in which knowledge was grounded in divine authority and absolutism; in the Enlightenment period, which saw the development of a kind of knowledge based upon reason that set about challenging traditional views; to contemporary times, dominated by technological information and relativism.

Activity

- Is there such a thing as a 'Knowledge Industry' society?
- Consider Blackler's typology and identify one example from your own knowledge base for each of the sub-divisions outlined
- Which type of knowledge is the most important?

Transition from manufacturing economy to knowledge production economy

Powell and Snellman (2004) indicate that the transition from manufacturing-based economies to those concerned primarily with knowledge production gathered momentum from the 1970s onwards. They suggest this was marked by the growth of computing and increased technological advancement, which made the shift from material outputs to knowledge-producing industries, an inevitable consequence. They further note that this technological period has resulted in unprecedented advances in intellectual capital and innovations, as indicated by increases in patents in developed Western economies. Alongside the technological growth, there has been global recognition of the benefits accrued and potential challenges to the emerging knowledge-based economy.

The Organisation for Economic Co-operation and Development (OECD) (1996) report on knowledge-based economies starts with the following supposition:

> The growing codification of knowledge and its transmission through communications and computer networks has led to the emerging 'information society'. The need for workers to acquire a range of skills and to continuously adapt these skills underlies the 'learning economy'. (p. 1)

The OECD (1996) report notes that this has resulted in an information-dense society in which investment in the skills of 'human capital' is essential if economies are to maximise on technologies for productivity. Olsen and Peters (2005) align this notion to the neoliberalist views of 'knowledge capitalism' espoused by Burton-Jones (1999, cited in Olsen and Peters, 2005) who argues that this shift can be liberating for the individual worker as distinctions between managers and workers and learning and the world of work become more blurred. He implies that this will lead to a growing economic imperative for a technologically skilled and educated workforce in which lifelong learning and knowledge acquisition are the norm alongside renegotiated industrial and organisational relations between workers, managers and companies. According to Olsen and Peters (2005) such neoliberalism is linked to seductive notions of global choice for individuals, organisations and multinational corporations alike, regulated by free-trade principles and minimal or absent state interference.

Curry (1997) argues that far from being a tool of empowerment and choice for knowledge workers, new technology has led to tensions between knowledge embodied in a machine or computer against that possessed by the worker and applied in production. He suggests that the emerging 'knowledge age' has not resulted in the worker gaining more control of the means of production, rather that they are more dependent on organisations to privatise, brand and commodify knowledge before it gains any significant exchange value, stating: 'I cannot walk into a store with my knowledge and "buy" something. Only value in its capital form (or immediately its money form) makes the world go round' (p. 8). He also asserts that the lived experience for the majority of knowledge workers is not characterised by creativity but based firmly in routinised technological procedures and specific application; becoming 'information mechanics' rather than 'brain workers'.

Olsen and Peters (2005) also identify concerns over the privatisation of knowledge and its consequences, noting that new power relations are being established as knowledge becomes capital: 'In the age of knowledge capitalism, the next great struggle after the "culture wars" of the 1990s will be the "education wars", a struggle not only over the meaning and value of knowledge both internationally and locally, but also over the public means of knowledge production' (p. 340).

Powell and Snellman (2004) note that debates have raged about whether organisational transformation (brought about by the shift from a manufacturing base to a knowledge-production industry) represents a move to more controlled work environments or to greater autonomy. They suggest that there is a clear dichotomy of opinion, in which there is either:

- understanding that a knowledge-production economy is a positive catalyst for a more empowered workforce, flatter management approaches and greater individual responsibility and flexibility

OR

- a belief that the emerging knowledge economy obscures some fundamental inequalities regarding wealth creation by dressing up exploitation and control of the workforce via the iron-fist-in-velvet-glove approach of quasi-consensual industrial relations

They assert that this dichotomy revolves around answers to one key question concerning supposed workforce reforms and links to productivity:

In a survey of 627 US establishments, Black and Lynch (2001) found that introducing high-performance workplace practices was not sufficient to increase productivity. When coupled with increased employee voice or profit-sharing practices, however, the introduction of workplace reforms had a positive effect on productivity. This finding goes to the core of the debate: Are these new practices intended to remake the organization of work to produce shared gains, or to increase productivity by increasing work output while the associated gains are skimmed off by those at the top of the (flatter) hierarchy? (p. 210)

Regardless of which philosophical position is applied in explaining the relative worth of the emerging knowledge economy, some key differences can be gleaned in relation to the older, more 'traditional' manufacturing economy.

Activity

Consider Tables 2.1 and 2.2 of apparent differences and disputed areas:

- Which do you agree with?
- Which ones do you have reservations about and why?
- Thinking about your own workplace, construct a table of key characteristics to determine if you belong to a knowledge-based organisation

---

Table 2.1   Traditional economy and knowledge economy: key differences

Traditional economy	Knowledge economy
• Market value based on scarcity of resource	• Market value based on abundance and application
• Location and time specific	• Virtual, global and not time-limited
• Relative stable pricing and volume	• Volatile pricing, highly dependent on context
• Requires low level of embedded knowledge	• Requires high level of embedded knowledge
• Based in physical human capital	• Based in cerebral human capital
• Machinery dependent	• Systems and process dependent

Table 2.2   Traditional economy and knowledge economy: disputed concepts

Traditional economy	Knowledge economy
• Routinised and mechanistic	• Creative and innovative
• Inflexible philosophy	• Highly flexible philosophy
• Alienating processes	• Empowering processes
• Rigid and hierarchical	• Evolving and democratic
• Worker subservience	• Worker autonomy
• Limited ownership	• Collective ownership
• Minimal staff development commitment	• Lifelong staff development commitment

Knowledge and professional autonomy

The emergent knowledge economy is based upon the key neoliberal suppositions of flexibility, accountability and active consumerism. New types of 'professional' worker roles are developing across occupational sectors, grounded in such notions. In the health and social care sector, the National Health Service (NHS) Plan (2000) illustrates the aspirations for a more flexible, consumer-based workforce.

The Plan sets out a framework for a ten-year period of investment and reform, including how the roles of many professionals will have to change significantly to accommodate a new consumer focus. The Plan (Delivering the NHS Plan: Next Steps on Investment on Reform, 2000, p. 8) articulates four main principles, comprising the following:

1   High national standards and clear accountability
2   Devolution of power and resources to the frontline to give health professionals who deliver care, the freedom to innovate
3   Increased flexibility between services and between staff to cut across outdated organisational and professional barriers
4   A greater diversity of service providers and choice for consumers

Taking each of these principles in turn, several paradoxes emerge. The assumption is that higher standards are achieved by the increasing use of accountability measures; this fails to recognise that greater accountability inevitably influences levels of professional autonomy and the 'freedom to innovate' when governed by an input–output approach to health care. Olssen and Peters (2005) suggest that this results-oriented approach underpins contemporary public service management in all spheres and is really about reducing 'quality' to economic production. They also argue that the concept of *'flexibility'* as outlined in the third key principle, refers primarily to sets of contractual norms and rules that organisations now serve and which govern them. They imply that this has had a disempowering effect on the status of professional roles:

Under liberal governmentality, the 'professions' constituted a mode of institutional organisation characterised by the principle of autonomy which characterised a form of power based on 'delegation' (i.e. delegated authority) and underpinned by relations of trust. Under neoliberal governmentality, principal-agent line management chains replace delegated power with hierarchical forms of authoritatively structured relations, which erode, and seek to prohibit, an autonomous space from emerging. (p. 324)

Far from encouraging new professional roles, Olssen and Peters (2005) argue that the resultant neoliberal application has sought actively to deprofessionalise occupational roles in many sectors. They contend that new contractual models of working involve tightly specified performance indicators that are at variance with a model of professionalism built around notions of rights, freedom and autonomy. They assert that the emergent neoliberal knowledge economy is characterised by activities that seek to deprofessionalise established occupational roles, involving:

- moving away from flatter, more democratically oriented, management structures towards hierarchical models that emphasise clearly defined, stringent specifications for effective job performance
- application of workload models that prioritise responsiveness to market demands and targeted outputs whilst reducing the capacity for professional autonomy
- erosion of the concept of earned rights bound up with classical notions of time-served professionalism. No professional group has wanted to have their practice dictated by anything other than their peers; however, market pressures encroach increasingly on the rights of professional groups for self-determination

Nixon (2001) argues that it is unhelpful to view the status of the professions as an either/or dichotomy between the new, highly managed professionalism, characterised in contemporary knowledge industries, against the past glories and virtuous amateurism of yesteryear. He asserts that the choice really concerns juggling with different versions of professionalism that are representative of different values and moral bases than those held previously. This involves recognising that the micro-narrative of professional 'worth' now needs to be tempered with a wider world-view underpinned by flexibility and adaptability to shifting economic contexts. He states that: 'Such values prefigure a professional re-orientation which requires of its practitioners a willingness to reconceive and radically readjust the relation between their own "small world" of professional interests and the wider public interests of the world "out there" ' (p. 179).

This upholds the direction taken in many public service industries, in which professional knowledge workers are expected to have the requisite level of expertise to maintain credibility, yet need to demonstrate a sophisticated level of reflexivity and adaptability in their everyday practice. In health care provision, the emergence of both Assistant and Advanced Practitioner roles epitomises this approach; both roles assume a specialist skills base and expertise at the appropriate level, whilst demanding that such workers operate ethically within a reflexive yet flexible framework.

Hardey (1999) suggests that today's health care context involves the 'proletarianisation' of professionalism, in which management divests professionals of their control and autonomy under the guise of meeting consumerist need through the provision of flexibility and choice. He argues that the realignment of the 'patient' to that of 'active consumer' can be associated with further deprofessionalisation, linked to notions of the 'expert patient'. Greater access to health information via the Internet has also contributed to an increase in lay scepticism about health professionals; well-informed health consumers now feel able to challenge the authority of esteemed professional knowledge bases. Hardey (1999) argues that health expertise is now defined holistically to encompass lay knowledge from a range of sources including patients, carers and family members. This shift, combined with increased scrutiny of health professionals' knowledge bases and claims to self-regulation, represents a challenge to the accepted wisdom of medical expertise and seeks to deprofessionalise by blurring the boundaries between consumer and expert.

Part of the demystification of health professionals' knowledge bases has involved the development of a raft of policies and protocols that aim to explicate contractual obligations between public service providers and the populations they serve. Examples abound, including a range of National Service Frameworks to which all health care providers are accountable. These are normative guidelines for professional practice, in which the practical mechanics of how health is delivered, in partnership with the consumer, is made explicit and public. Neoliberal intentions of standards, accountability and flexibility are made clear from the outset, in which the:

> Government is committed to building a new NHS; faster, fairer and more convenient for patients; a health service fit to face the challenges of the new Millennium . . . . National Service Frameworks set out plans, based on the evidence of what works best, to ensure that in future these standards of care are available to everyone. (National Service Framework for Coronary Heart Disease, 2000, p. 2)

Checkland (2004) implies that such tightly explicated guidance can actually lead to greater professional autonomy, rather than eroding existing expertise. She uses Lipsky's notion of 'Street Level Bureaucrats', whom Lipsky defined as: 'public service workers who interact directly with citizens in the course of their jobs and who have substantial discretion in the execution of their work' (Lipsky, 1980, cited in Checkland, 2004, p. 955). Checkland asserts that many health care workers are such street level bureaucrats, maintaining a unique level of autonomy through individual professional–patient interactions, regardless of the stringent requirements demanded for the upkeep of their wider professional credibility. She calls into account notions of active consumerism in health care, pointing out that whilst the 'client' or 'patient' has evolved theoretically into a 'consumer', they really have little choice over whether, where or how they access health care services.

Despite misgivings in some sectors, ever-increasing public accountability measures reflect this changing priority towards a consumer-led knowledge economy. According to Olssen and Peters (2005), neoliberal knowledge economies distrust traditional professional infrastructures, viewing much of old-style professionalism as self-serving, driven by individual opportunism and operating primarily from behind closed doors. This has spawned a variety of explicit accountability measures that place emphasis on market processes and quantifiable success indicators and outputs. They note a shift away from a bureaucratic model of accountability towards a consumer-driven model:

- 'The bureaucratic model' of accountability, in which success is measured in terms of process rather than direct output, with standards set and regulated by those with relevant professional expertise
- 'The consumer model' of accountability, in which success is measured in terms of fulfilling pre-set contractual obligations and targets. Contractual obligations are set via market systems and pricing arrangements, with specified reward and punishment incentives for target achievement

The relationship between a knowledge economy and professional autonomy is complex and subject to perceptions concerning both pitfalls and possibilities of ascendant neoliberalism. The following scenario highlights some key questions for consideration:

Scenario

Joe Smith is the manager of a new Children's Centre within a local authority setting. He is in discussion with a range of social and healthcare providers about the best way to provide appropriate staffing for the new integrated services unit.

(Continued)

He sees nothing wrong with employing a mix of cross-sectoral para-professionals to provide an affordable service that will have tangible benefits for sustaining the five key facets of the Every Child Matters initiative concerning: being healthy; staying safe; experiencing enjoyment and achievement; making a positive contribution; achieving economic well-being.

He hopes that this will enable a more flexible approach that can go beyond traditional daytime hours. The existing professionals believe that the intention to extend to an out-of-hours service, staffed primarily by paraprofessionals, is the start of a 'slippery slope' to erosion of their professional worth and will have dire longer-term outcomes. All parties concerned have reached an impasse.

Questions

- Should the drive towards affordable and flexible provision override professional concerns?
- Will using para-professionals enhance the service?
- What are the key tensions and how could these be resolved?

Chapter summary

This chapter has examined the emergence of a knowledge industry and the key facets underpinning its development. The role played by ideology, both historically, and in determining boundaries of acceptable knowledge is significant; despite debates about its intrinsic worth, ideology provides a framework that influences world views and provides the 'commonsense' of any given age. Knowledge provides the vehicle for this sense-making and is aligned to the demands of any ascendant economy. In past analyses, such knowledge production has been linked to information and skills needs of manufacturing economies; yet as Edwards and Usher (2001) note, the movement towards a knowledge economy per se has liberated its production from many of the conventions of natural sciences that prevailed in the manufacturing economy boom years from the post-World War II period until the 1970s.

According to Powell and Snellman (2004) the transition to a knowledge-production economy gained pace alongside the growth of new technologies and advancements in computing. This spawned the emergence of a neoliberal view of 'human capital' in which knowledge production equates to global choice, free market economics and lack of state intervention. Opinion is divided concerning the relative merits of the knowledge economy; Curry (1997) argues that the new worker roles still rely primarily on organisations to control the means of production through the privatisation and branding of knowledge. Drucker (1993) disputes that a knowledge-production emphasis divests workers' of power, arguing that individuals are now at the centre of this post-capitalist economy due to the ideas held in their heads and their absolute power over timing of its release.

The relationship of knowledge to professional autonomy is another highly contested area. Olssen and Peters (2005) define how neoliberal approaches of accountability and flexibility have resulted in perceived asset stripping of many professional bases in public sector services. In the health care sector, the policy rhetoric of the new knowledge economy espouses flexibility, putting the patient first and modernisation of traditional roles. This has led to an apparent drive for pragmatic responses that enhance service provision. The shift has been sold to the public as a set of practical responses that result in some efficient solutions, yet the underpinning approach epitomises a neoliberal ethos not a set of apolitical actions as claimed.

Sources of further reading and exploration

Books and journals

Burton-Jones, A. (1999) *Knowledge Capitalism: Business, Work and Learning in the New Economy*. Oxford: Oxford University Press.

Chomsky, N. (1989) *Necessary Illusions: Thought Control in Democratic Societies*. London: Pluto.

Drucker, P. F. (1993) *Post-Capitalist Society*. New York: Harper Business.

Katz, S. N. (2002) 'The Pathbraking, fractionalized, uncertain world of knowledge', *Chronicle of Higher Education*, 49 (4): B7–B11.

Lam, A. (2002) 'Alternative societal models of learning in the knowledge economy', *International Social Sciences Journal*, 54 (171): 67–82.

Lipsky, M. (1980) *Street Level Bureaucracy: Dilemmas of the Individual in Public Services*. New York: Russell Sage Foundation.

Web

Hayek, F. (1937) 'Economics and knowledge', *Economica IV*. Available at: www.hayekcenter.org/friedrichhayek/hayek.html

3

ASSUMPTIONS

Stella Jones-Devitt and Liz Smith

This chapter examines the nature of assumptions. It helps the reader to identify commonly held assumptions and establish how these gain validity and endure over time. Types of assumption and representation are discussed alongside issues of reality and certainty. The reader is introduced to notions of shifting contexts and multiple realities, and possible implications for professionalism and practice.

Chapter aim

- To examine the nature and validity of assumptions

Learning outcomes

After studying this chapter, you should be able to:

- identify commonplace and enduring assumptions
- critically analyse physical and perceptual assumptions
- appraise the relationship of shifting contexts and multiple realities to the manufacture of assumptions
- explore the relationship of assumptions to professionalism

Identifying assumptions

Before exploring why assumptions develop and prevail, it is important to consider their nature and initial purpose. The Critical Thinking Competency Standards devised by Paul and Elder (2005) highlight some of the key issues regarding the nature of assumptions and presuppositions. They define assumptions and presuppositions as: 'beliefs we take for granted' (p. 25). They then suggest that all thinking can only be judged as sound, or otherwise, dependent on the initial assumptions underpinning the thoughts per se. Paul and Elder (2005) unpack the 'dispositions' necessary to be both aware of one's own assumptions and those of others, indicating that successful performance is indicated by the following ten outcomes:

1 being able to identify accurately one's own assumptions and those of others
2 making assumptions that are reasonable and justifiable in the context of both situation and evidence
3 making assumptions that have widespread consistency
4 having awareness of the tendency to use stereotypes, prejudices, biases and distortions in their reasoning, alongside identifying the same within others' thought processes
5 being able to state accurately the assumptions underlying inferences made by both self and others; then assessing whether the assumptions made are justifiable
6 recognising that assumptions occur primarily at unconscious and/or subconscious levels
7 recognising that the human mind seeks to hide unsustainable assumptions in order to maintain a preferred belief system or to pursue selfish objectives
8 being able to seek out such unjustifiable assumptions, hidden within these unconscious and/or subconscious levels
9 accurately identifying assumptions contained within specific subjects, disciplines and texts
10 identifying assumptions embedded in the concepts and theories selected to study

Some clarification of how assumptions influence inference is required in order to make the fullest sense of Paul and Elder's (2005) assertions. The supposed link between assumptions and inferences is illustrated by the following example:

If assumptions are based upon beliefs concerning something that is taken for granted or presupposed, it could be assumed by public health practitioners that everyone wishes to have 'good health'; this view is grounded in the belief that people should seek to maximise their potential.

Inferences are based upon intellectual acts which draw conclusions that something is true in light of something else being true, which then affects the level of certainty of our initial conclusion. For instance, if using the above public health example, it may be 'inferred' that somebody choosing a potentially health-damaging behaviour is either (a) ignorant of the health facts about the activity, or (b) has very low self-esteem (otherwise, they would inevitably undertake activities which seek to maximise their potential for good health). These options would be underpinned by the 'assumption' that everybody wants good health. Whether this inference is based upon sound beliefs is then open to further speculation, dependent upon the assumptions of those undertaking the speculation! The following figure illustrates dilemmas arising from the assumption–inference process (see Figure 3.1).

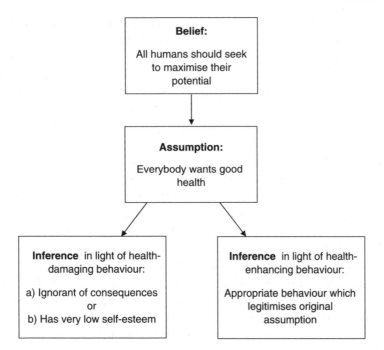

Figure 3.1   The assumption–inference process in public health

Janoff-Bulman (1989, cited in Dekel et al., 2004) defined a World Assumptions Framework in order to gain further understanding of individuals' enduring beliefs about their world. She suggests that assumptions can be clustered into the following three essential categories:

1   Benevolence of the world
    In which the 'impersonal world' is viewed through events outside of the individual's direct terms of reference; hence, a positive skew on assumptions in this category, leads to expecting more good things to occur rather than bad, and vice-versa.
2   Meaningfulness of the world
    In which peoples' beliefs about distributive justice reside; this can be further divided into three distinct sub-sets: (a) 'justice' – a belief that people deserve what they get and get what they deserve (b) 'controllability of outcomes' – a belief that people can actively control their own world outcomes by means of engaging in appropriate behaviours (c) 'randomness' – grounded in the belief that there is no point in trying to rationalise what happens to people as outcomes appears to be determined by chance alone.
3   Self-worth
    Again, split into three further sub-sets: (a) self-worth – comprises the degree to which individuals' perceive themselves as good, moral and decent human beings (b) self-controllability – the degree to which individuals' perceive themselves as engaging in right and proper behaviours that ameliorate vulnerability to negative outcomes (c) luck – in which individuals perceive themselves to be protected from ill-fortune despite traits in character or subsequent behaviours.

According to Ginzburg (2004) once a set of assumptions is formed, there is a strong tendency to preserve the status quo of the sum total of a particular beliefs system; thus, any new information received is assimilated and absorbed within an existing framework rather than adapting the beliefs in accordance with the new information; this supports the assertion by Paul and Elder (2005) that to become a higher-order thinker, it is essential to be able to recognise such maladaptive processes that underpin many commonplace assumptions.

Berman (2001) describes the process of becoming aware of assumptions made, as being part of true 'wisdom', and almost based upon developing a consciousness about subliminal thoughts and beliefs. He suggests that individual world views are informed by personal assumptions that then become self-fulfilling and part of an elliptical process: 'We project our unconscious assumptions onto the world of reality. We are both the creator and product of our assumptions' (p. 431). He goes on to suggest that many personal statements and behaviours are probable, rather than certain; failure to recognise such uncertainty leads to jumping to inappropriate conclusions. Berman (2001) indicates that it is therefore more productive to replace assumptions of certainty with assumptions of probability instead.

Table 3.1 provides an analysis of Paul and Elder's (2005) original assertions about Assumptions Performance Indicators; the critique recognises that World Assumptions have wider resonance for how the individual constructs, orders and prioritises their own beliefs accordingly.

Activity

Please consider the following questions in light of the assumptions debate discussed earlier:

- Can you have a 'disposition' to explore assumptions?
- Can you legitimise assumptions as suggested, via 'sound reasoning and evidence'?
- Are your 'World Assumptions' relatively fixed?
- Now consider Table 3.1 which analyses Paul and Elder's Assumptions Performance Indicators
- Is the analysis valid?
- Can you draw any conclusions about the assumptions underpinning the analysis?

Table 3.1 Analysis of assumptions performance indicators

Performance indicator	Analysis
1 Being able to identify accurately one's own assumptions and those of others	Difficult to fulfil if assumptions are at subconscious/unconscious levels?
2 Making assumptions that are reasonable and justifiable in the context of both situation and evidence	Perhaps, who decides what is 'reasonable' etc. is the crucial factor?
3 Making assumptions that have widespread consistency	Links to World assumptions outlook, rather than situated?
4 Having awareness of the tendency to use stereotypes, prejudices, biases and distortions in their reasoning, alongside identifying the same within others' thought processes	Difficult to pursue; people are often only aware of applying biases and distortions when identified by others.
5 Being able to state accurately the assumptions underlying inferences made by both self and others; then assessing whether the assumptions made are justifiable	Often exist as self-fulfilling prophesies; difficult to determine legitimacy of others' thoughts
6 Recognising that assumptions occur primarily at unconscious and/or subconscious levels	If subliminal, how can such recognition occur?
7 Recognising that the human mind seeks to hide unsustainable assumptions in order to maintain a preferred belief system or to pursue selfish objectives	Reification of the 'mind' as separate from socially constructed person?
8 Being able to seek out such unjustifiable assumptions, hidden within these unconscious and/or subconscious levels	How, if subliminal? Relationship to cognitive dissonance?
9 Accurately identifying assumptions contained within specific subjects, disciplines and texts	Assumptions embedded are often explored in appropriate literature; how 'accuracy' is determined is problematic.
10 Identifying assumptions embedded in the concepts and theories selected to study	Selecting tools of analyses that mirror personal notions of World Assumptions?

Physical and perceptual assumptions

Berman (2001) suggests that assumptions are often dressed up as facts; he indicates that this process can involve using three levels of abstraction as listed below:

1 First-order abstraction – in which the person experiences the phenomenon directly and empirically, thus is selecting directly from a non-verbal fact. For example, experiencing a physical illness.

2   Second-order abstraction – in which the person 'describes' the event experienced in words or verbally, thus this is a one-stage-removed abstraction of the non-verbal fact. Using the illness example, this could involve the person describing symptoms to a General Practitioner (GP).

3   Third-order abstraction – in which the person experiencing the phenomenon is further removed during the abstraction. In the above example, the GP writes up the case notes of the person's illness experience which can then be accessed by a variety of other workers.

He contends that directly observable experiences form stronger associations that help to legitimise the justification for personal assumptions and presuppositions. Assumptions grounded in visual information have endured over time. From the Middle Ages onwards, a sense of aesthetics and beauty has been informed by spatial reasoning and notions of symmetry. As Flew (1984) notes, the term 'aesthetics' derives originally from Greek and was used initially to define the study of sense experience; by the mid-eighteenth century, it had developed into a set of assumptions about visual beauty in both nature and art.

Perkinson (2005) outlines how physiognomic assumptions began to underpin representational works of art during the Renaissance period; this constituted a move away from visual representations based around groups towards depicting likenesses and traits of individuals instead. He describes the prioritising of physical likeness over iconography as: 'a sign marking the triumph of the self-conscious individual of the Renaissance over the anonymity and corporate identities of the Middle Ages' (p. 507). He also asserts that assumptions grounded in visual representation are always context-dependent, indicating that an artefact judged in the present day would be considered differently in accordance with the assumptions of the prevailing culture. Using portraiture as an example, he states:

The number of ways in which an image can resemble its subject are potentially infinite, and the degree of resemblance that a viewer expects to find between image and subject is also infinitely variable. As a result, the criteria by which one gauges concepts such as "likeness," "resemblance," and "realism" are always historically and culturally contingent. (p. 508)

Historically, further visual assumptions have prevailed through a range of sources, including the use of 'tromphe l'oeil': literally to trick the eye, in which artists like M. C. Escher in the early twentieth century confused the viewer with impossible physical perspectives and structures that challenged assumed wisdom about spatial reasoning, gravity and reality. *Tromphe l'oeil* was preceded by the development of physiognomy. Its main advocate in the late eighteenth century was a Swiss priest J. G. Lavater, who offered a new 'scientific' theory that involved assessing internal character traits from the shape and form of external appearance; primarily, this involved critiquing the face and head and was deemed to be a partly aesthetic, partly philosophical activity. This process spawned a range of ancillary 'pseudo-sciences', with phrenology being worthy of particular note.

Phrenology was developed by a German physician, Franz Josef Gall, in the nineteenth century. He believed that relative strengths, weaknesses, dispositions and abilities could be determined by measuring the contours of individuals' heads; contending that these measures were indicative of the underlying cerebral contours that possessed particular attributes. Selby (1993) notes that Gall prioritised his attention upon a detailed configuration of the human head, increasing the number of areas he attributed to specific aspects of cerebral functions that he thought were indicative of underlying human personality traits; indeed, in early-twentieth-century America, head 'readings' became popular and it was not uncommon for couples to have joint readings prior to marriage in order to assess their compatibility!

Context and the manufacture of assumptions

Health and social care presuppositions, assumptions and inferences have prevailed throughout history. The following chronology details some of the key historical phenomena that contributed to popular beliefs of their time, alongside still informing humans' socially constructed belief systems today.

1   ANCIENT CIVILIZATIONS – underpinning assumptions comprised the following:

- Ideas of 'Natural Order' in society
- Order determined by physical difference in sexes. Males provided form, women provided the matter
- Early notions of dualism
- Amoral hierarchies

A natural pecking order, or fixed hierarchy, was viewed as desirable and necessary for a thriving society; men were unquestionably intellectually superior, with women being primarily vessels for carrying future generations.

2   EARLY CHRISTIANITY – underpinning assumptions comprised the following:

- Adam and Eve phenomenon
- Women as moral wreckers and 'temptresses'
- Men as 'tempted'
- Women's use-value primarily determined by fertility
- Evil significance of menstruation

A time when all deferred to a higher authority; women were still viewed as inferior creations manufactured from cast-off matter of men's construction; additionally, women were perceived to be seductresses and distractions for men, and they were also defined solely by their ability for reproductive tasks.

3   RENAISSANCE PERIOD – underpinning assumptions comprised the following:

- Rigidly prescribed lives for both men and women
- Recognition of a public/private domain of existence
- Families characterised by virtue and piety of men and subservience of women
- Family life ruled by authority of husband, church and state
- Contrasting options for men and women

By now, men were characterised by their relation to wider 'public' society; women only viewed within the private sphere and, as still lesser beings, expected to be subservient to church, state and, particularly, their husbands.

4   THE ENLIGHTENMENT – underpinning assumptions comprised the following:

- Period of questioning of ideas (thought and culture) emerging from late seventeenth and eighteenth centuries
- Signified a break from absolutism in politics, religion and social life
- 'New science' phase – linked with Descartes, Galileo and Newton
- A move away from religious explanations of social existence towards developing an understanding of human nature
- Growth of liberal thought and thinkers
- Growth of middle classes and entrepreneurial capitalism
- Growth of female dissension?

A period that challenged the place of 'divine intervention' as the sole arbiter of people's fate; the growth of an emerging middle class also led to a growth of free-spirited thinkers who were unafraid of being irreverent; female dissention did exist, yet it was often unheard or valued.

5   ESSENTIALISM – underpinning assumptions comprised the following:

- Obsession with exploring human 'nature' and trait categorisation
- Rise of essentialist perspectives in medicine, psychology and biology
- Manifested by: Darwinism and Eugenics, Evolutionary Psychology, Socio-biology
- Key notion of binary opposites: that it is evolutionary productive to have separate female/male ways of thinking

This marked a drive for discovery and exploration relating to human behaviour that built upon the foundations laid within the Enlightenment period; The previously-immutable idea of creationism was now challenged by notions of evolutionary development that sought to distil the very 'essence' of human existence.

6   NEO-SCIENCE – underpinning assumptions comprised the following:

- Authenticity of 'Natural Sciences' and focus upon biological orientation
- Emphasis upon internal workings and bodies as systems of engineering (Descartes – Cartesian analysis)

- Ill health – mechanical failure; mechanical failure necessitates direct repair of damage
- De-contextualisation: growing interest in biological hazards (e.g. Miasma Germ Theory)
- No real understanding of why some individuals/groups are more sick than others
- Focus upon material rather than mental dimensions of illness
- No framework for assessing the subjective experience of illness

This approach mirrored the obsession with manufacture and systems of production. The key assumption concerned viewing the body as a Fordist production-line machine that could be engineered, repaired, dissected and maintained by medics and other 'scientists', in order to keep it from dysfunction.

7   EUGENICS MOVEMENT – underpinning assumptions comprised the following:

- Term first used by Sir Francis Galton in eighteenth century, who studied the role of factors under social control that could either improve or impair the development of future generations
- Modern eugenics is concerned with two basic issues: negative eugenics – the discouragement of perpetuating the 'unfit'; positive eugenics – the encouragement of perpetuating those humans of healthy, intelligent and highly moral character
- First half of the twentieth century saw zealous application of extreme eugenic posturing via holocaust solutions of Nazi Germany to enforced sterilisation of the insane in the US
- A eugenic theme runs through some recent forms of genetic screening and surveillance. Examples include pre-conception screening, foetal assessment and the Genome Mapping project

Building from the engineering metaphors of the neo-scientific period, the early twentieth century Eugenics movement was grounded in the premise of both manufacturing human perfection, alongside ameliorating imperfect functioning and bodies. This drive gathered momentum via the right-wing supremacist political view gaining popular credibility across Europe at the time.

Many contemporary health and social care policies and practices are grounded in inferences emanating from assumptions about lifestyles and the risks attached to specific health behaviour choices. For example, the work of actuaries, in which insurance policies and premiums are set, is based upon a series of complex lifestyle and longevity projections. However, Parks (2003) describes how many of the assumptions made about health insurance risks are grounded primarily in 'one-size fits all' approaches that do not allow for individual differences:

Are we sometimes so convinced our assumptions about financial planning are "right" that we forget some clients do not fit the mould and need to take a different path? Where many advisors fall into trouble is when they encounter clients who, due to health issues, occupations, finances or foreign travel or residence, do not fit the norms of our business. Unfortunately, many advisors fail to adjust their set of assumptions to meet the unusual needs of these individuals. (p. 8)

Activity

Please read the following three 'risky scenarios' about assumptions and the relationship to risk, and consider:

- What 'risky' behaviour is taking place in these scenarios?
- How might you view things differently if you were:

  (a) The person concerned
  (b) A friend
  (c) A health or social care professional

- How can these scenarios be altered for the better?
- What assumptions underpin each scenario?

Risky scenarios?

Scenario one: Sue (53) is a community worker in the voluntary sector working with people considered to be 'vulnerable'. She is officially paid for 30 hours work per week, yet she 'loves her job' and does 50–60 hours regularly. Until recently, Sue has thrived on being busy, yet she now experiences intermittent chest pain and is always tired. She has visited her GP to discuss her health concerns but as yet no obvious causes have been identified to explain her symptoms. Sue lives with her daughter, Jane, who is about to go away to university but is really worried about leaving her mother alone in the present circumstances. Because of her busy working life, Sue does not have many other friends outside of work, so does feel a bit isolated at times; she is also adamant that she does not wish her own situation to jeopardise her daughter's future plans.

Scenario two: James (19) is a first-year physiotherapy student, who also plays county-level badminton. He aims to fulfil his ambition to become a sports physiotherapist once he has completed his studies. Because of his sports-training regime, he finds it quite difficult to comply with all the academic demands made and has not achieved the grades expected during the first year. He has also been officially warned about his attendance on the programme; he perceives that he needs to 'get away from lectures' as much as possible in order to undertake the training necessary to compete in his sport at high level. Outside of scheduled teaching sessions, he has little time to socialise with his fellow students, who perceive him to be a 'badminton bore' and a liability who is not really interested in physiotherapy as a future career. Recently, he has developed flu-like symptoms that cannot be shaken off; this has prevented him from training properly and is causing him considerable anxiety as he has an important match coming up.

Scenario three: Ethel (82) enjoys life to the full; despite losing her beloved Frank two years ago, she still manages to get to bingo, go shopping and keep her home clean in the way that she and Frank liked. She has two grown-up children whom she is very close to and who visit her regularly, three grandchildren and one great-grandchild on the way; Ethel is very excited about the prospect of being a great-grandmother yet she overheard her son and daughter discussing how they had concerns about her ability to look after herself now in her own home; she is terrified of the idea that they are going to 'put her away' into a care home, yet feels too upset to even discuss it and is worried that it may prompt them into action. She acknowledges that she has become more forgetful recently – last week, a neighbour had to tell her that her she had left her front door wide open all night – yet she puts this down to 'slowing down a bit' and is only to be expected in somebody of her age.

Assumptions and professionalism

The term 'professional' is both evolving and contested. It can be used to describe particular groups in society within any given period; however, group membership of professions varies according to timescale and cultural location. Middlehurst and Kennie (1997) suggest that there are some key assumptions which inform a set of beliefs associated with being 'a professional'. They assert that such assumptions determine a set of professional characteristics, comprising the following:

- A claim of mastery over a particular skill, discipline or vocation
- Advanced learning and requisite higher qualifications
- Higher-order intellectual skills
- Autonomous practice and discretion, whilst adhering to specific codes of practice and ethical frameworks
- Specific attitudes to work, clients and peers involving dedication, trust, reliability, flexibility and creativity

---

Activity

Please consider the above list of assumed professional characteristics:

- How do these characteristics relate to your own profession?
- Do they reflect accurately an overarching concept of professional character?
- Which of the assumed characteristics are fixed and which most likely to change?
- Given the rise of 'associate' and 'para' professionals in health and social care, how will they fit within an assumed set of characteristics?

Paul and Elder (2005) contend that assumptions (sound or otherwise) provide a foundation for inferences to be drawn; when applied to explaining human behaviour, these can become reinforced, leading to fixed ideas or stereotyping. This approach permeates notions of specific professions in health and social care and beyond, and attaches stereotypical behaviours accordingly. Long et al. (1997) imply that exposure to stereotypes is inevitable and forms part of early childhood sense-making processes. In helping to provide a sense of location, problems occur in relation to power. Long et al. (1997) contend that: 'it should be remembered that stereotypes are not neutral, we attach inferior and superior values to them and they are historical formations which have an inherent power dimension linked to questions of control' (p. 253).

Activity

Consider your own profession:

- What stereotyping surrounds it, if any?
- Where do these views come from?
- Are they helpful?

Clearly, it may be useful to differentiate between the social stereotyping of certain groups, in which, as Long et al. (1997) suggest: 'because of asymmetrical power relations, the ability of those being stereotyped to define themselves is constrained by the dominant discourse' (p. 253) from the privileges incumbent in professional stereotyping. Class, gender, race and sexuality provide examples of more pejorative forms of stereotyping that are grounded in assumptions and presuppositions that seek to oppress and marginalise; conversely, professional stereotyping already confers a privileged position within social hierarchies and is more likely to be about sustaining a position of power, than it being denied. The benefits of professionals within the social infrastructure are often viewed positively, as Middlehurst and Kennie (1997) note:

> There are numerous benefits to society and economy of 'professionalism' and of those activities commonly associated with professionals. For example, professional skills supply necessary services and, if delivered at a consistently high level, provide competitive advantage for the economy. The granting of professional independence and discretion, particularly when exercised with responsibility, dedication and creativity, is a significant economic benefit since it obviates the need for close, detailed and costly supervision and monitoring of service delivery and overall performance. (p. 65)

Whilst Middlehurst and Kennie (1997) present a compelling rationale underpinning some of the more positive assumptions associated with 'professionalism', it is worth noting that within specific domains, including health and social care, a set of professional rivalries and 'pecking orders' still differentiates expertise and implied status.

Chapter summary

This section has considered principles underpinning the construction of assumptions and the relationship to the development of robust critical thinking skills. Some of the competencies advocated by Paul and Elder (2005) in relation to assumptions, presuppositions and inference have been explored, alongside whether a 'disposition' for recognising personal limitations and prejudices can be cultivated. The influence of both physical and perceptual assumptions has been examined and acknowledgement given to the socio-cultural location of such ideas. Within health and social care, the association of assumptions to risk-taking and longevity has been examined, alongside further analyses of key beliefs underpinning 'professionalism' and, by extension, stereotyping.

Sources of further reading and exploration

Books and journals

Berman, S. (2001) 'Opening the closed mind: making assumptions, jumping to conclusions', *Etc.*, 58 (4): 429–439.

Elder, L. and Paul, R. (2002) 'Distinguishing between inferences and assumptions', *Journal of Developmental Education*, 25 (3): 34–35.

Gray, J. (2003) *Straw Dogs: Thoughts on Humans and Other Animals*. London: Granta.

Stangor, C. (ed.) (2003) *Stereotypes and Prejudice: Essential Readings*. Hove, East Sussex and Philadelphia: Psychology Press.

Web

The Critical Thinking Community: comprehensive US site covering resources, seminars, training and position papers. Some interesting insights into the nature of assumptions. Available at: www.criticalthinking.org/

Critical Thinking on the Web: Tim van Gelder's unique repository of a range of subjects and insights related to critical thinking. Available at: www.austhink.org/critical/

The Skeptic's Dictionary. A site full of resources concerning eclectic beliefs, deceptions and delusions. Available at: http://skepdic.com/

4

THE NATURE OF EVIDENCE

Peter Draper and Liz Smith

This chapter explores the nature of evidence and addresses different ways of understanding its role in health and social care. The chapter begins with a description of the privileged position that 'evidence' is given in contemporary health and social care, particularly in the context of the 'evidence based practice' movement. It then outlines certain key concepts associated with scientific ways of thinking, including empiricism, induction, deduction, falsification and positivism. Next, limitations of the scientific approach are discussed, drawing on the work of philosophers Dilthey and Gadamer. Throughout the chapter, debates about the nature and usefulness of different types of evidence are related to underpinning philosophical perspectives, and debates about the nature of evidence are linked to the broader issues of critical thinking.

Chapter aim

- To explore the nature of scientific and 'non-scientific' approaches to evidence, and to think critically about them

Learning outcomes

After studying this chapter, you should be able to:

- identify key concepts associated with scientific and 'non-scientific' types of evidence
- outline a number of critiques of scientific approaches to evidence and link these to their respective philosophical perspectives
- appraise the relationship of types of evidence to critical thinking

Evidence: where's the problem?

This chapter examines the nature of evidence. Once, discussions about the nature of evidence might have been considered an obscure branch of philosophy, but now the concept of evidence occupies centre stage in public policy, affecting everyone who works in health and social care or uses these services from time to time. For example, arguments about how the safest way of vaccinating babies against measles, mumps and rubella, or the availability of drugs to treat breast cancer, can be reduced to arguments about evidence; protagonists in debates like these often have different views about what types of evidence are legitimate, how evidence can be interpreted, and how it should feed into the decision-making of service users, professionals and politicians.

Activity

Consider a range of different circumstances in which you use evidence, either at work or in some other aspect of life.

- identify as many different types of evidence as you can
- reflect on the key differences: can you discern any reasons for such difference?

These debates cannot simply be resolved by coming to an agreement about what counts as evidence and deciding to base practice solely on those interventions for which the strongest evidence can be found. Health and social care is provided within a political and economic context. Practices must not only be measurably effective: they must also be economically viable; hence, claims from both the Social Care Institute for Excellence and the National Institute for Health and Clinical Excellence that they derive good practice from robust evidence. This is why the Research and Development Strategy of the National Institute for Health and Clinical Excellence prefaces its commitment to 'rigorous assessment of the best available evidence' with a reminder that its overall function is to: 'provide national guidance on the clinical and cost effectiveness of treatments and care' (p. 3).

The concept of evidence is complex in ways that are not always acknowledged in the literature. Sackett et al. (1996) suggests that evidence based medicine is 'the conscientious, explicit, and judicious use of current *best evidence* in making decisions about the care of individual patients' (italics added). This definition hinges on the words 'best evidence', and Sackett et al.

go on to explain that this is:

> By best available external clinical evidence we mean clinically relevant research, often from the basic sciences of medicine, but especially from patient centred clinical research into the accuracy and precision of diagnostic tests (including the clinical examination), the power of prognostic markers, and the efficacy and safety of therapeutic, rehabilitative, and preventive regimens. External clinical evidence both invalidates previously accepted diagnostic tests and treatments and replaces them with new ones that are more powerful, more accurate, more efficacious, and safer. (p. 71)

Activity

Read Sackett et al.'s (1996) definition of evidence:

- Identify any assumptions it might contain
- What are the limitations of this definition?
- What are the circumstances in which it might be useful?

This definition provides a useful starting point for exploring the nature of evidence, because it has frequently been cited in the wider literature of the evidence based movement.

In principle, there might be many different kinds of evidence, depending on the kind of question being considered. The evidence needed to support an explanation of an historical event such as the disappearance of the dinosaurs is likely to be quite different from that needed to explain how children learn to read; and by extension to the wider arena of health and social care, the evidence sought to explain the presence of a bruise on a child will differ from that obtained to support the effectiveness of a treatment for cancer. However, Sackett et al.'s definition of evidence reduces it to narrow 'scientific' terms (without explaining what they means by science in this context), and then focuses it still further by invoking the concepts of clinical relevance and patient centredness.

A further feature of Sackett et al.'s definition is its lack of equivocation. Evidence will have a double effect which can be summarised as 'out with the old' (as previously accepted tests and treatments are found to be invalid), and 'in with the new' (as powerful, more accurate, more effective and safer treatments take their place). There is no acknowledgement of the need for interpretation in this process, and the possibility of doubt is not entertained. The assumption is that there are 'facts of the matter', and the powerful tool of scientific evidence will enable us to establish what they are. There are no shades of grey in this definition, no ifs, buts or maybes, and the possibility that conflicting evidence may be discovered is not entertained.

The third interesting feature of Sackett et al.'s definition is the implied belief that the world works according to a linear model of causality in which 'a' leads to 'b', which in turn leads directly to 'c'. One of the paradoxes of evidence-based practice is that professional work is done within organisational structures, and organisational behaviour is extremely resistant to change. For all sorts of reasons, people are often happy to persist in old patterns of practice, and simply giving information about innovative modern approaches is rarely sufficient stimulus to engender change.

Scientific approaches to evidence

Detective stories and television crime shows offer an excellent starting point for thinking more widely about the nature of evidence and how it is used in science. In popular fiction a good deal of energy is expended on gathering clues. In forensic police shows, clues often take the form of the collection of fingerprints, DNA and other physical traces from the crime scene. The next task is to work out who committed the crime. Usually there is more than one suspect, so the detective has to match the clues to different possible scenarios and may search for further evidence and interview suspects. Finally, the truth is dramatically revealed! The best detectives can spot clues that others have missed, but they also have a better attitude: Sherlock Holmes (Conan-Doyle, 1887) is successful because he approaches each case with an open mind and does not jump to conclusions or draw false inferences. He fearlessly follows the logic of the case: 'Eliminate the impossible and whatever remains, no matter how improbable, must be the truth'.

The processes of science are not quite as clear as in the fictional world of the television detective, but there are some interesting parallels, and some of the key concepts of the scientific approach will now be considered.

'Empiricism' is one of the basic doctrines of science. Empiricists believe that knowledge can easily be distorted in all sorts of ways. Biases and pre-suppositions, habitual ways of thinking, undue deference to authoritative figures, received wisdom, and conclusions drawn from false premises, can all lead to mistaken views of reality. The way to avoid this is carefully to observe and document the phenomena we are interested in, thereby ensuring that our conclusions have a sound basis in observation and experience.

Quine (1988) defines the concept of empiricism in a formal way as:

> the theory (1) that all concepts are derived from experience, i.e. that a linguistic expression can be significant only if it is associated by rule with something that can be experienced, and (2) that all statements claiming to express knowledge depend for their justification on experience. (p. 269)

For example, to develop the detective analogy, we can only be sure that the statement 'the butler killed the cook with the candlestick' is true if we can find physical evidence such as finger prints, or if we obtained the testimony of an eye witness.

Empiricism seems a very modern doctrine, but it has a long pedigree. Francis Bacon, a philosopher in the seventeenth century, was one of the first to describe it (Oakley, 2000). In his book 'The New Organon', published in 1620, Bacon attempted to clear away 'the intellectual debris or existing assumptions which distort the perceptions and cloud the judgement of the would-be philosopher' (Jardine and Silverthorne, 2000: xix). Bacon suggested that human attempts to understand the world were commonly influenced by sources of systematic error which he called 'idols'. Bacon identified four of these: idols of the tribe, the cave, the marketplace and the theatre.

'Idols of the tribe' are errors of perception born of habit and preconception. For example, for many years it was believed that the orbits of the planets around the sun are circular, whereas in fact they are elliptical (Ladyman, 2002). In health care for example; neonatal paediatricians firmly believed that premature babies could not experience pain as their nervous system was not sufficiently developed but it is now known that despite their immature development they do feel pain (Carter, 1994). 'Idols of the cave' are errors 'introduced by each individual's personal prejudices and attachment to particular styles or modes of explanation' (Jardine and Silverthorne, 2000: xix). Arguably professional stereotyping in health and social care is as a result of this type of thinking. 'Idols of the marketplace' are the confusions that may arise from imprecise use of language. For example, the word 'strike' can refer to a blow with the hand, or industrial action in which workers withdraw their labour. There are many words and phrases that mean different things in different specialisms and professional groupings in health and social care and this is also clear in patient and client's language. Finally, 'idols of the theatre' are biases that might result from flawed philosophical methods.

Bacon hoped to avoid the influence of these idols through the empirical method of systematic observation and experimentation, and it can be seen that modern advocates of evidence based practice such as Sackett (1996) mirror his approach very closely. It is very common for evidence based practice to be presented in a way that contrasts it favourably with older approaches based on ritual, tradition, uninformed clinical expertise and the like, which stand in the place of Bacon's 'idols'; and the modern advocate of evidence based practice stands foursquare in the empirical tradition.

Activity

- Apply an example of each of Bacon's 'idols' to your own area of professional practice experience
- Consider whether empirical approaches to evidence could remove these influences

---

It can therefore be argued that the concept of 'evidence' that underpins evidence based practice is deeply rooted in the empirical tradition within the philosophy of science, and its roots have been traced to the work of Francis Bacon in the seventeenth century. However this is not the end of the story: as our analogy of crime fiction shows, it is not sufficient simply to collect evidence, for one also needs to ask the right questions and draw the correct conclusions. The concepts of induction and deduction therefore need to be explored.

In its simplest form, induction is the view that, if we make a sufficient number of detailed, careful and relevant observations about something we are interested in, we will eventually be justified in claiming that the conclusions we draw are valid beyond our personal experience and are in fact generally true. This way of extrapolating from numerous, single observations, has been extremely influential in health and social care. As they go about their work, all health and social care professionals observe what is happening, and build up a store of personal experience. This store of personal experience is then often used when making decisions about the care of individual clients and we could say that professionals who do this are using an inductive approach.

Another example of induction in practice is the use of aspirin as an analgesic. The pain relieving properties of this drug were not discovered as the result of a modern randomised, controlled trial, but through many years of observing its success in individual patients and eventually reaching the conclusion that it is effective in treating certain kinds of pain. The problem with both of these examples is that, no matter how many observations an individual makes, he or she is still likely to be biased or simply to draw false inferences, and the trial and error of inductive practice has, in the past, led to practices and treatments that would seem bizarre today. Despite these reservations, 'induction' is one of the major ways in which evidence is used in day-to-day practice.

Activity

- Consider something from your practice which you would judge to be based on induction as described above. Do you think that the thinking behind it may have been biased? If so, why?
- Do you think that Health and Social Care Professionals can often be biased in their inductive judgments because they have a different perspective to patients/clients? If so, does this matter?

Induction gives one account of how generalisations are derived from observation, but induction in itself is not a complete or entirely satisfactory account of how science might work. It is quite possible, for example, that two scientists working inductively might generate quite different theories to explain some phenomenon. In these circumstances, there needs to be some way of choosing between the theories. Alternatively there may be just a single theory, but there needs to be a way of finding out if it is an appropriate one. It is possible to ask whether the theory is simple, whether it seems to be powerful enough to explain lots of individual observations, and most importantly of all, whether it enables prediction, with some degree of success, what might happen in hypothetical future circumstances. That is to move beyond induction and consider a process that philosophers call deduction. Ladyman (2002) defines deduction as:

> Deduction is inference in accordance with the laws of logic. A deductively valid argument or inference is one where it is not possible for the premises all to be true while the conclusion is false. A sound argument is one that is valid and where all the premises are true [and hence so is the conclusion]. (p. 264)

The idea is that induction provides a tentative theory that seems to help with understanding of something, but the theory should not be taken at face value and needs evaluating. For example, the social psychologist Solomon Asch developed a theory that when a person who is in a group with other people is asked to report a simple judgement, such as stating whether two lines on a card are the same length, he or she will be influenced by their perception of what the group thinks. On the basis of this theory, a deduction could then be made: if Asch's theory is true, we might expect to be able to find instances of people's judgement being affected by group membership. An example of this could be the influence of previous blood pressure recordings on the recording of an inexperienced member of staff or the influence of another colleague's concerns regarding the nature of a child's injuries on a decision regarding a possible non-accidental injury case.

A possible explanation therefore of how science works could be as follows: first here is an inductive phase in which thorough observation is made and other empirical data are collected. On the basis of these observations, a theory is proposed. The theory is then evaluated by deriving predictions from it through a process of deduction. Finally there is a further phase of observation in which evidence is sought to validate the deduction. If this search is successful then perhaps we can assume that the theory is a correct one. This entire process is known as hypothetico-deductivism. This process has also been linked to theoretical approaches to decision-making in health and social care particularly in relation to diagnostic reasoning (Harbison, 1991).

An important question remains, and that is, how precisely does the evidence function to test a theory? One approach might be to suggest that the purpose of the evidence is to support the theory being evaluated. For example, if there is a theory that all swans are white, further examples of finding white swans could add to the verification, for every time one was spotted it would be considered as one more piece of evidence in support of the theory.

An alternative approach, however, is known as falsification an idea that was developed by Popper (1959). Popper argued that instead of looking for evidence to support theories, evidence should be sought to undermine them; hence, the best theories will be those which can most successfully withstand attempts to prove that they are false. Thus, the way to test the theory that all swans are white is not to look for more white swans, but to go hunting for non-white ones.

Positivism is a philosophy of science which flourished in the nineteenth and early twentieth century and has had a central role in shaping modern scientific enquiry (Brown, Crawford and Hicks, 2003). Its 'founder' Auguste Comte considered that all science, and therefore research, can provide an objective understanding of any phenomenon. Comte had been impressed by the spectacular advances of the natural sciences and technologies of the eighteenth century (Giddens, 1976), and he regarded the extension of science into the study of human life as a direct outcome of the march of human understanding towards 'man' himself.

Von Wright (1971) has identified three core characteristics of positivism. The first is 'methodological monism'. This is the view that, irrespective of the subject matter, scientific methods provide the most valid, powerful, objective and useful approach for generating knowledge. The second characteristic is the view that the natural sciences, and in particular mathematical physics, set a standard with which all the development of all other forms of knowledge can be compared and against which they can be judged.

The third characteristic is the most important for the present circumstances, and it concerns the overall function or goal of science. Von Wright suggests that for positivists, the goal of science is essentially to discover cause-and-effect relationships, to express these as laws, and then to use these laws to explain individual events. This is known as 'explanation'.

At one level positivism is a very modern doctrine. It expresses very precisely the underpinning values of the evidence-based movement with its carefully graduated scale of research methods, at whose pinnacle resides the systematic review of randomised controlled trials; but at another level, it is a doctrine with a long history. Indeed it can be traced back to Francis Bacon and his revolutionary ideas about empirical knowledge.

The primary concern of Bacon and his contemporaries had been natural phenomena, which is why their work was described as natural philosophy. Towards the end of the nineteenth century, however, attempts were made to extend the scope of Bacon's empiricism beyond nature, and into the world of human beings and their interactions, human cultures and societies.

As Howard (1982) explains, Comte argued that just as laws had been found to explain the interaction of elements in nature, so they could be found for the interaction of people in society, and the physics of mechanical movement was complemented by a 'social physics' of human beings.

The scientific use of evidence

This section has addressed the nature of evidence particularly as it is used in science. It has been shown that in science, evidence usually takes the form of empirical observations and measurements of the phenomena of interest to the scientist. It is argued that science has inductive and a deductive phases. During the inductive phase, the evidence generated by observation and measurement is used to develop tentative theories about the way the world works. In the deductive phase, these tentative theories are tested, and those that successfully survive attempts to demonstrate that they are false live on to fight another day.

The whole purpose of this process is to demonstrate the causes of things, to show why and how things happen, and hopefully to develop laws which will aid prediction and enable control of what will happen in the future. This is known as explanation. For the positivist, there is no reason in principle why this approach may not be as successfully applied to understanding of the social world as it is to the physical phenomena of nature: this is precisely the logic of the evidence-based movement, as it is sometimes advocated.

In the next section, various objections and criticisms of this view of science and its relevance will be considered.

Criticisms of scientific approaches to evidence

The scientific approach to evidence can be criticised at a number of levels, but one of the most effective critiques is based on the work of the German philosopher Wilhelm Dilthey (1833–1911). Dilthey's work is interesting because it cuts at the roots of positivism at the level of its most basic assumptions.

Dilthey's particular field of interest was not the natural sciences, but a group disciplines which he called the 'geisteswissenschaften'. The literal translation of this term is 'sciences of the spirit'. The geisteswissenshaften include history, anthropology, sociology and other disciplines which study the various ways in which human beings create cultures and societies, and the artefacts such as books, buildings, bodies of knowledge and other cultural products which are created by human cultures. A more modern term for geisteswissenschaften might be 'cultural studies'. Dilthey argued that knowledge and understanding of human phenomena was impossible through positivism. He therefore argued for interpretivism where the emphasis is on the lived experience of social reality (Brown, Crawford and Hicks, 2003).

The overall goal of Dilthey's work was to describe the methods through which valid knowledge could be created in these disciplines. He argued that the character of such knowledge was fundamentally different in its scope and purpose from that of the natural sciences. Dilthey accepted that the proper subject matter of the natural sciences is the many phenomena which constitute the natural world: this might include the interaction of chemical elements, the nature of forces such as gravity and electricity, and the evolutionary pressure of natural selection; and he also accepted that the goal of these sciences was to describe these phenomena and then to formulate laws to account for the relationships between them. In other words, the fundamental purpose of the natural science was to explain.

Dilthey contrasted the explanatory function of the natural sciences with the goal of cultural studies, which was to understand it. The difference between explanation on the one hand and understanding on the other might seem rather semantic, but it is an important one to understand because it has significant implications for our understanding of the nature of evidence. There is a sense in which the study of natural phenomena is 'disinterested', at least in principle: for example, when an astronomer looks at the moon through a telescope, the act of looking does not change the fundamental nature of the moon itself. However, it is much more difficult to sustain this argument when the object of study is the product of a human culture because we are also human beings, living in a culture and a history, and this profoundly shapes the understanding of other people and their way of life.

Dilthey's work on the nature of understanding was further developed in the later twentieth century by another German philosopher, Hans-Georg Gadamer who, in his book Truth and Method, tried to establish 'discover what is common to all modes of understanding' (Gadamer, 1975: xix). Gadamer rejected the view that science and the scientific method are wholly adequate to all of the truth (Lawn, 2006): in other words, that science holds the franchise on understanding.

Gadamer was particularly critical of the importance attached to scientific method, by the advocates of science. Traditionally, scientific method is described as a way of neutralising presuppositions and prejudices, or what Bacon might have called 'idols'. Scientific method is necessary because, for the natural scientist, presuppositions are like 'lice in the hair', and must be eliminated at all costs (Peters, 1974). Thus, the ideal scientific thinker is like a blank slate, or a purely open mind onto which the data \of his research can inscribe unbiased knowledge.

Gadamer argues that understanding simply does not work in that way, and he outlines an alternative view based on the concept of the 'horizon'. In everyday usage, the horizon is the range of vision that includes everything that can be seen from a particular vantage point, or perspective. It defines what is seen, and also defines the 'limits' of what is viewed.

Activity

Gadamer defines the 'horizon' as everything that can be seen from a certain point of view.

- Identify key elements that determine your outlook on the world from a professional perspective
- How might this differ from a service user perspective?

The concept of the horizon provides Gadamer with a powerful metaphor which he uses to explain the process of understanding. For Gadamer, both the person who is trying to understand something, and that which they are trying to understand, exist within an horizon that can be understood as being defined by their historical and social situation. For example, the horizon of personal understanding might be constituted by gender, race, educational background, religious beliefs, political views, social roles, occupation and so on. It is impossible to leave this behind when trying to understand something new, because it is what provides a personal perspective on the world. In other words, it is simply impossible to step out of a personal horizon (although of course it will change as a person's view moves). Thus, the world cannot be seen from another's point of view simply by an act of the will. Rather, understanding is what happens when, to use Gadamer's term, a personal horizon fuses with that of the object of interest to form a new, more comprehensive horizon.

Conversation offers a good model of the way in which understanding occurs. Palmer (1987) considers that in a true conversation, one person does not simply ask questions of the other in order to discover what they think, for this would not be conversation but interrogation. Equally however, two people are not described as being in dialogue when one is haranguing the other without listening to their response. True conversation demands a quality of openness from both participants: an attempt by each to discover what the other is saying; and preparedness from each to place their own prejudices at risk through openness to what the other has to say.

Gadamer's approach to understanding offers a way of understanding the role and function of evidence, which differs quite markedly from the scientific, positivist account. In the first instance, it is holistic rather than reductionist. Evidence will not be seen as 'data', isolated factual fragments divorced from their context, but as a series of interlocking elements within a larger whole whose meaning is derived from its relationship to that whole. A simple professional example illustrates this point. Blood pressure is recognised as an important parameter when evaluating a person's health, and blood pressure readings may be taken during health screening, of following surgery, or in other circumstances. However, an individual blood pressure reading carries very little meaning on its own, but only when related to other relevant information. Its meaning emerges when it is seen in the context of a 'set' of data including previous blood pressure readings and records of pulse monitoring, together with knowledge of the person's immediate situation.

A second implication is that understanding always takes place against a background of what is already known or believed, and may therefore be influenced by previous experiences, practical professional or life skills, world views and existing knowledge. As such, understanding may never be an entirely 'rational' affair in which a tipping point is reached when the balance of evidence approaches a certain critical mass, but may also have an intuitive dimension. This has clear implications for concepts of evidence: in other words, what evidence is perceived to be. It will also determine to a large extent what type and level of evidence are found to be persuasive, and how evidence will be used in order to persuade other people.

Chapter summary

This chapter has explored the nature of evidence, discussing the concept's use in health and social care and tracing its history through the development of modern science. The nature of evidence is a philosophical problem but it has very practical implications for contemporary contexts. The advocates of evidence-based practice base their concept of evidence on a scientific model, and assume that evidential facts will enable us to sift through the variety of practices and interventions to determine which are best. The unspoken assumption is that professionals will then modify their practice to reflect these findings.

Evidence based practice appears to be a very modern approach to health and social care, but the conceptual foundations on which it rests can be traced to the Enlightenment and the work of philosophers such as Francis Bacon. These conceptual foundations include empiricism, which stresses the importance of observation, experience and objectivity; induction, which suggests that knowledge is built up from a series of observations until valid generalisations can be made; deduction, where conclusions are made on the basis of logical inference; and falsification, Popper's theory of science which explains how theories are tested against evidence. We have also discussed positivism, the view that the methods of the natural sciences are universally valid and can be applied to the social world with just as much success.

This scientific, or 'positivistic' account of the role of evidence is extremely powerful and influential, but not without its critics. Dilthey criticised the validity of applying scientific methods to human cultures and societies, distinguishing between explanation, which he considered to be the function of science, and understanding, the proper function of cultural or social studies. Dilthey's work was developed by Gadamer who developed the concept of the 'horizon' to explain the importance of a perspective, or world view, and its essential function in all attempts to observe and theorise about the world.

Sources of further reading and exploration

Books

Gadamer, H. (1975) *Truth and Method*. London: Sheed and Ward.
Ladyman, J. (2002) *Understanding Philosophy of Science*. London: Routledge.
Popper, K. (1959) *The Logic of Scientific Discovery*. London: Hutchinson.
von Wright, G. (1971) *Explanation and Understanding*. London: Routledge and Kegan Paul.

Web

www.scie.org.uk
www.shef.ac.uk/scharr/ir/netting/
www.york.ac.uk/inst/crd/

Section 2

KEY THEORETICAL TOOLS OF CRITICAL THINKING

5

POLITICAL IDEOLOGIES

Stella Jones-Devitt and Liz Smith

This chapter considers some of the major concepts and debates associated with development of political ideology. It provides an overview of key ideas, starting from an examination of some notable historical developments underpinning political theorising to more specific notions identified under the rubric of 'left-wing', 'centre-ground' and 'right-wing' thinking. The chapter covers these three main strands of political ideology, assisting the reader through specific exercises and activities to assess their relative impact upon policy analysis, policy formulation and subsequent service provision. It does not attempt to encompass all divergent political viewpoints but seeks to capture the overarching themes that prevail, thus providing some critical perspectives and application in relation to health and social care.

Chapter aims

- To provide an overview of key ideas underpinning major political ideologies
- To promote reflection upon the relevance and value of political ideologies in the context of health and social care

Learning outcomes

After studying this chapter, you should be able to:

- identify key concepts associated with principal political ideologies
- critically discuss contemporary issues in health and social care using a range of contrasting political perspectives
- evaluate the use of political ideologies as critical thinking tools in the context of health and social care

Principal political ideologies

The boundary between what constitutes an ideology as opposed to a political doctrine is somewhat malleable. Heywood (2003) argues that they are not necessarily one and the same thing; ideology does not always have an active component whereas politics is underpinned completely by notions of power-gaining. Once elected, the democratic mandate for policy-making (see Figure 5.1) then becomes the active output of political thought processes.

When applied to political theory, ideology helps to focus some of the sense-making from an already established position of choice. As Freeden (1996) notes, ideology can be used to help shape broad political perspectives in relation to a cluster of core, adjacent and peripheral beliefs; hence, not all of these facets have to be included for a political doctrine to be recognised as belonging to an overall ideology. For example, two political doctrines that claim to hold broadly concurring ideological underpinnings are socialism and social democracy. Socialism is underpinned by notions of collectivism, in which the needs of the greater good prevail; universalism, in which the commitment to freely available state-owned services is enshrined; common ownership, in which a dissembling of private wealth built around a competitive capitalist economy is seen as both desirable and essential; all of this is grounded in a commitment to the creation ultimately of a classless society.

Table 5.1 highlights some of the differences between socialist and social democratic approaches, whilst still sharing a broader overarching ideology. Social democracy, whilst sharing broad notions of upholding collectivist approaches, differs in both what it views as the 'greater good' and how this can be achieved; hence, social democracy prioritises distributive justice approaches in which state-sanctioned provision is available to all, but in which the right to services has to be earned or justified; it also favours a mixed economy infrastructure as being the best way to obtain maximum efficiency for the most people; all of which is then grounded in relative equality which provides incentives for self-betterment in pursuit of the greater

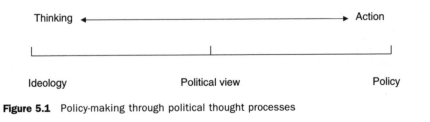

Figure 5.1 Policy-making through political thought processes

Table 5.1 Socialism and social democracy – underpinnings of political ideology

Socialism	Social democracy
• Total collectivism	• Partial collectivism
• Universalism	• Distributive justice
• Common ownership	• Mixed economy
• Equality	• Relative equality
• Enduring	• Modernising

Figure 5.2 The linear axis of political perspectives

good, rather than via a classless society which social democrats perceive as de-motivating. As Alcock et al. (2000) note, social democrats believed that: 'Only a minority of disadvantaged people . . . still fell outside of the advantages conferred by a transformed and welfare-oriented post-capitalist society' (p. 235). Socialism is also premised on enduring values that remain relatively unaltered, whereas social democracy is built upon notions of responsiveness and reform; indeed, it is often viewed as the optimum political model for modernisation and flexibility.

Socialism and social democracy are often placed along a left-of-centre ideological perspective, although the supposed continuum embracing left, centre and right-wing politics can be challenged as being both too simplistic and unreflecting of an evolving political climate. Heywood (2003) notes that the notion of 'wings' to describe the spectrum of political opinion first emerged from the French Revolutionary period, when during the first meeting of the Estates General (1798), the Monarchists and reactionaries sat together on the right whilst the revolutionaries appeared directly in opposition, upon the left. This spawned the notion of presenting political perspectives as being plotted along one long linear axis (see Figure 5.2) from left to right.

This continuum presents a very clear cut picture of the range of political perspectives, yet is rather unrepresentative of the conceptual complexities and shades of opinion. For example, anarchism is difficult to place upon a one-dimensional continuum; its core values of liberty and anti-statism appear to place it towards the extreme margins of the political right, however, anarchism also values anti-materialism and absence of hierarchy as key facets placing back towards the far left. The growth of 'single-issue' political organisations such as environmental pressure groups and animal rights lobbyists has also made a one-dimensional perspective largely redundant.

This linear perspective works best only when viewed as a one dimensional facet linked to economic assessment. In historical terms, a linear view was most effective during the highly polarised times of revolution and emerging capitalist economy. This provided a clearly differentiated picture between the ruling/landed classes who held wealth, power, and ownership of the means of production against those who had no power, no ownership and only their physical labour as their primary resource. Right wing-interests were initially represented by aristocracy and by rich land owners and industrialists, who believed in an innate physical order, rigid social hierarchy and the sanitising influence of manual labour upon the 'lumpen' masses.

This contrasted with those on the left who viewed the existing elitist hierarchy (or 'bourgeois' ruling classes) as being detrimental to all but a privileged few in society, alongside a belief that hard manual labour in pursuit of unshared profit resulted in a de-humanising process and alienation of such individuals (proletariat) from their essence as creative and social human beings. In a republication of his critique of the nineteenth-century industrial family, Engels (1986) suggested that: 'In the industrial world, the specific character of the economic oppression burdening the proletariat is visible in all its sharpness only when all special legal privileges of the capitalist class have been abolished and complete legal equality of both classes established' (p. 105).

Along the continuum are grouped various 'isms' with communism and socialism viewed as the ideas of the political left, liberalism occupies the centre ground whilst conservativism and fascism offer a right-wing perspective.

However, a one-dimensional linear view does not allow for flexibility and change along the spectrum; moreover, it denies the influence of context and the ascendancy of certain political values at any given time. For example, Callinicos (2003) notes that there has been a global shift of political theorising primarily through the influence of the US political right during the latter part of the twentieth century and beyond: 'It is indeed a peculiar kind of internationalism that leaves peoples free to choose the "single sustainable model of national success" – American-style laissez-faire capitalism' (p. 29). Hence, the adoption of hitherto right-wing concepts of freedom, liberty and individualism by mainstream parties of the supposed left and centre ground. Whilst still claiming left and centre-ground credentials, these political parties now embrace key facets of a neoliberal economy without further thought as part of a 'modernisation' process. In the UK context, the Labour Party's eschewing of Clause 4 of its constitution (concerning collective ownership) on return to power in 1997, is indicative of just how far to the right the socio-political landscape has moved.

Heywood (2003) indicates that the development of liberalism provides another vivid example of how historical context mediates political meaning: as a product of the post-Enlightenment period, liberalism in the nineteenth century epitomised the valuing of the nascent industrial market economy whilst seeking limitations to state's powers of interference in capitalist development. This positioning occurred in conjunction with a commitment to safeguarding civil liberties that recognised the supreme importance of the individual; characterised by the new industrial entrepreneurs of the so-called rising classes. Heywood (2003) contends that modern liberalism has shifted its view of the state from seeing it as being very inhibiting of individual freedoms, towards one of accepting that an effective state can help to ameliorate the excesses of a capitalist/post-capitalist economy that still result in different forms of injustice and denial of individual self-fulfilment.

Given the shifting socio-political context, it is more productive to identify some common areas that do allow certain 'isms' to be clustered together and to also offer differentiation across several key themes. Table 5.2 represents some of the key categories for differentiating between the main political perspectives; it is by no means an exhaustive list and many more categories could be added. It is built upon an 'IDEA' approach; namely Ideology, Democracy, Economy and Authority as applied to each political wing.

Application of political ideologies to contemporary issues in health and social care

The UK public sector provision is underpinned by apparent apoliticism, in which pragmatic concerns outweigh any notions of policy-making driven by application of overt political ideology. However, on further scrutiny, the influence of political ideology in the health and social care domain does have a marked effect upon: general policy underpinnings; the approach taken in prioritising need; the resultant service provision; the role played by individuals in maximising health and social status. As Hunter and Marks (2005) note, within an NHS culture, political commitment at the highest level is required to move the NHS away from being a sickness service. They state: 'It is not enough to say that all that is needed is to refocus the NHS from being a sickness service to a health service, and that the way to do this is to come up with tougher targets and penalties for missing them' (p. 7).

Table 5.2 Political wings: key differences

Principle	Left wing	Centre ground	Right wing
Ideology	Views ideology as leading to false consciousness; inoculates workers from the real source of oppression	Liberals view ideology as repressive and damaging to notions of individualism and free will	Regards ideology as dressed-up scientific repression, based on spurious and abstract notions of human reason rather than based in reality
Democracy	The left endorses democracy, provided it is based on inclusive popular participation alongside a wish to bring economic systems under wider public control	The centre ground considers democracy from an individualistic perspective; hence, it welcomes the rights of individuals to express views through the democracy of the ballot box – provided there is a fair and transparent process that prevents tyranny	Accepts that a limited democracy can offer a framework for individual expression, provided that core values, traditional infrastructures and hierarchies can be protected from subversion
Economy	Views common ownership and social equality as central economic tenets; an ideal left-wing economy relies upon state collectivism and central planning	Considers a mixed economy built upon a capitalist infrastructure as most desirable; engages with individuals via competition and market rewards. Accept limited state interference	Supports laissez-faire economics and private enterprise as the best means of providing the individual with the most efficient choices; the new right sees unregulated global capitalism as the only way forward
Authority	Views existing authority with suspicion, as inherently linked to oppression of the masses and privilege for the few; supports authority underpinned by collective decision making and accountability	Believes that authority rises from the bottom up via consent of the governed; limited authority is therefore desirable in order to provide a modicum of rationality and public accountability; tensions are recognised between the need for societal authority and preservation of individual rights	Considers that authority emerges from natural order and individual merit; although essentially hierarchical, sees authority as beneficial to promoting respect, providing a sense of social order and for enhancing social cohesion

Although boundaries have been blurred in relation to the traditional tri-partite political spectrum of left, centre and right-wing notions, key differences can still be discerned and applied to a contemporary health and social care context. Table 5.3 provides a summary of the key differences within the domain, as according to contrasting political perspectives.

Table 5.3 Political ideologies applied to health and social care

Doctrines	Political ideology	Policy underpinnings	Health and social care approach	Health and social care service provision	Perceived role of the individual	Key strengths	Major criticisms
Left wing	Communist socialist	Collectivist	Prioritises the elimination of inequalities; views material redistribution of wealth as the key issue	State funded and fully nationalised; free, universal provision	Individual has minimal control over own health and social status	Attacks causes of social and health ills at macro policy level; prioritises state infrastructure	Unrealistic in the global marketplace; too top-down and 'nannying'
Centre ground	Communitarian liberal social democratic	Social justice	Focuses upon a combination of both behavioural and materialist factors	Mixed economy provision of public, private and voluntary sector involvement; means tested for ability to pay	Individual has some responsibility for own health and social status alongside wider material factors	Provides a safety net for those who need it, whilst recognizing that most individuals can take some responsibility for own health status	Fails to recognise ethical dilemmas of adopting a 'carrot and stick' approach
Right wing	Fascist conservative	Anti-collectivist libertarian	Asserts that a 'free market' economy should provide all necessary opportunity for individuals to pursue own health and social care needs	Wholly-funded through the private sector; no free service provided, nor deemed necessary	Individual has absolute responsibility for own health and social care	Advocates the rights of the individual; eschews state interventions in health and social care	Lacks humanity as it prioritises the strongest and ablest; fails to recognise differential contexts

---

Activity

Consider Table 5.3 and the explanations for left, centre ground and right wing application to health and social care.

- Which of the political ideologies has had the most influence on your practice?
- Which political perspective (if any) will shape the future of service provision in the foreseeable future?
- Will your profession need to alter if priorities are changed?
- How might this have a direct impact on your role?

Left wing

This perspective embodies both communist and socialist views, although the discernible global economic drift to the political right means that more dilute forms of socialism are much more likely to hold credence in contemporary contexts. As Sekulic (2004) notes there has been a redefinition of many state identities, marked by the diminishing influence of harder-line communist views throughout the second part of the twentieth century. This has continued into the present day, with overt examples of systems under-pinned by communist principles often reduced to the status of 'other' and constructed as 'rogue states'. The key policy driver of the broad left is a commitment to collectivist ways of working in which the needs of both state and the greater good prevail over individual rights and responsibilities.

This approach sees material and structural inequality as key by-products of an ascendant capitalist economy. In policy terms, Alcock et al. (2000) suggest that this translates into tackling material deprivation as the main priority for enhancing health and social status. This involves the redistribution of wealth as the best means possible to achieve optimum health and social wellbeing for the greatest number; for once the primary cause of social malaise is attacked, the symptoms of poor health and low social status will inevitably decline.

A left-wing political ideology is committed to state-funded and fully nationalised health and social care services, which are completely free of charge at the point of delivery and provided universally for all, regardless of income and means. Although upfront costs are absent, services are paid for through progressive and incremental taxation approaches in which those earning the most, pay more in proportional terms for services provided. Any profit imperative is an anathema to this perspective unless such 'gains' are about elevated quality of life rather than financial reward. As Jochelson (2005) notes, this approach seeks to alter health and social ills at macro-policy level, taking the view that the individual has minimal control over their own health and social status. It argues that unless the prevailing social infrastructure is built around addressing the amelioration of poverty, reduction of structural and material inequalities and the pursuit of human need not wealth acquisition, it is inevitable that health and social care provision will be concerned primarily with tackling symptoms rather than causes.

A major strength of this perspective is that it provides an ideological framework that has the scope for large-scale analysis; it can look at the causes of population malaise through its critique of macro-policy processes, thereby offering widespread solutions at organisational, national and global levels. The philanthropy underpinning a left-wing perspective is also viewed as one of the key weaknesses in its armoury. Jochelson (2005) suggests that the 'nanny state' criticism still has resonance, via the perception that a socialist ideology is too idealistic and cumbersome for the fast-moving and fragmented global marketplace in which competition not consensus is the norm; hence, the top–down collectivist approach advocated by the left appears out of kilter with the libertarian freedoms expected by individuals and modern economies.

Centre ground

This perspective provides a fusion of ideas ranging from notions of Communitarianism, championed by the US academic Etzioni (1995) to quasi-liberal intentions underpinning European models of social democracy, to the relativism of 'Third Way' political theorising that, according to Giddens (1998) has become the dominant hybrid term of Western political analysis. The common denominator concerns the application of a social justice approach in which individual rights and responsibilities, and their relationship to community cohesion, play a central role. Heywood (2003) notes that a social justice ethic is built traditionally upon the premise of: 'a morally defensible distribution of benefits or rewards in society' (p. 146) yet this has become increasingly difficult to define in an evolving mixed economy context. Within the health and social care domain, this relates to a focus on a combination of factors that affect and determine health and social status. Like its left-wing counterpart, centre-ground ideology views material and structural factors as key variables influencing quality of life; yet there is also acknowledgement of the part played by individual behaviours in contributing to overall wellbeing. This recognises that individuals have some responsibility and obligations to stay well, alongside the community's role in seeking to improve the wider material infrastructure for all of its citizens.

Centre-ground approaches locate health and social care service provision within a mixed economy ethic in which public, private and voluntary sectors are all involved. Due to the social justice policy underpinnings, services are not free to all; replaced instead by means-tested access according to ability to pay. There are also other moral costs involved in this approach, in which citizens have duties and civic obligations to keep themselves as well as possible through their own responsible actions. This introduces the dichotomy of the 'deserving' and 'undeserving' and is arguably what contemporary versions of social welfare are based upon; in which those unwilling to help themselves receive a basic safety net service whilst those citizens willing to behave responsibly are recognised and rewarded appropriately.

A key strength of this approach concerns the recognition of the individual alongside broader structural factors; an accommodation of interests in which moderation and moral actions and social imperatives fit well with contemporary health and social care practices and provision. This strength can also be viewed as a weakness due to an obfuscation of wider socio-economic factors by focusing on individual rights and responsibilities. A social justice approach often fails to recognise the ethical dilemmas of using a carrot and stick approach. Alcock et al. (2000) note that those who can't or won't make the 'right choices' or buy into an appropriate set of core community values, are punished disproportionately regardless of personal context.

Right wing

Heywood (2003) documents that a right-wing perspective can range from extreme right fascist notions of leadership, nationalism and colonialism; to neoliberal views of individualism, globalisation and entrepreneurial ism; through to paternalistic conservativism in which tradition, state authority, hierarchy and organic development are prized. Right-wing policy prioritises the freedoms of the individual, taking an anti-collectivist, libertarian approach in which choice, liberty and competition are central features for wellbeing. This ideology asserts that the most effective health and social care will be provided by a free market economy, which left to its own devices, should provide all necessary opportunities for individuals to pursue their own health and social care needs. This perspective diminishes the role of the state in providing health and social care services; such libertarian provision results in no state-run health and social care institutions, relying instead on wholly private sector funded resources and services that are available for individual consumers to choose.

This view is crystallised by Hanson (2006) when discussing available incentives for effective self-care within the UK:

The tax funded system of health care in this country has become counterproductive. It does not give any incentive to prevent or avoid diseases. As a result, not only should the provision of health care be decentralized but also opened up to market forces . . .

This means that the patient acquires full consumer power since he is put in control of all health expenditures on his behalf. The crucial point of a consumer-driven healthcare system will be the direct link between personal lifestyle and individual control of health expenditure with fully informed consumers. (p. 3)

Alcock et al. (2000) suggest that this is consistent with an overriding belief in the right of individuals as active consumers to take responsibility for their own wellbeing without further state interference or regulation. Its primary strength revolves around the seductive notion of ensuring the rights of the individual to self-determination whilst eschewing state intervention as ineffective and disempowering. Weaknesses concern an intrinsic lack of humanity, founded on prioritising the strongest and ablest whilst ignoring differing social contexts that exacerbate structural inequalities.

Political ideologies as critical thinking tools in health and social care

Understanding the way policy and practice is shaped by contrasting political ideologies can offer new insights into both the status quo and future developments. As an example, Allsop et al. (2004) argue that the concept of 'active consumer' is now one that prevails strongly in health and social care policy rhetoric. By applying a left-wing critique, the critically thinking practitioner can note that the concept of 'active consumer' would be seen as merely obfuscating wider structural inequalities through a process of inoculation; this contrasts with right-wing notions of consumption as espoused by Hanson (2006) which imply that regulatory frameworks and state interventions into personal wellbeing are both divisive and unhealthy. The centre-ground perspective utilises a distributive justice approach to active consumerism, falling between the left and right dichotomy, indicating that maximising upon opportunities to maintain and improve wellbeing is both an individual moral obligation and a societal responsibility; hence, each plays its part in preserving an essential level of socio-economic community cohesion.

As Alcock et al. (2000) note, there are some key health and social care policy areas for further scrutiny, for example – the role of the state offset by individuals as 'active consumers'; the emergence of new professional roles; regulation and accountability; public and private sector funding tensions; impact of technological advances – all of which can be unpacked effectively by practitioners using a range of political ideologies as critical thinking tools. The critically thinking practitioner needs to be able to navigate a well-considered course through competing explanations, as the following exercise portrays:

Activity

- See if you can determine the political base of each of the following explanations
- Identify at least two further issues drawn from your own professional experience. How would each contrasting political perspective differ when explaining the same issues?

1 The re-emergence of Tuberculosis (TB)

   A: The resurgence of TB can be allied to two key factors. One relates to the group of citizens still living in relative poverty and dealing with all of the health problems that poor quality of life entails. The other factor concerns those citizens who do not look after their health to its best effect, and therefore don't comply with their responsibilities to both their families and the wider community. Solutions lie within creating a better quality of life for those who need it, and to make all citizens accountable for maximising their health potential.

   B: TB is caused by poverty: pure and simple. The fact that TB is now re-emerging merely reflects the growing gap created between rich and poor. The only solution is to produce a more equal society by redistribution of income and overall capital.

2 Supposed increase of anti-social behaviour due to poor parenting skills

   A: Yet another sign that families are being coerced into making decisions by the Nanny State. Individual families must have the freedom to make their own choices and deal with the consequences of their own actions. The fact that Government is trying to minimise choices (thus forcing parents to comply) is another vivid example of state interference over individual liberty. The solution is to abandon the one-size-fits-all approach orchestrated by the state that de-motivates people by destroying personal choice. Anti-social behaviour would be significantly reduced if individual family units could decide for themselves as active consumers within a free market economy rather than as passive clients in a state-led society.

   B: It is morally and socially desirable that all responsible parents teach their children about basic rights and wrongs. Without decent parenting underpinned by wider social obligations, community cohesion is compromised and endangers us all. The Government needs to persuade those who do not comply that their actions are selfish and damaging for the greater good of all citizens.

3 Rise in Coronary Heart Disease (CHD) incidence in women

   A: Clearly women have been too used to the state taking responsibility for their health whenever possible. This has resulted in an inability for most women to take control over their lives and health. At the top end of the scale, there are women chief executives who are stressed constantly by having their hands tied by increasing levels of state-sponsored regulation and intervention. At the bottom, is a whole group of women who are totally dependent on state handouts. They have no motivation to improve their own health because they know that the state will always cover their mistakes, and often provide them with council housing at no cost, subsidised by the efforts of others.

B: Women are often the poorest in society yet have the most responsibility – no wonder CHD is on the increase! Unequal pay, discriminatory employment conditions and lack of quality childcare provision lead to high levels of stress for working-class women. The ethos of free market thinking does nothing to help the majority of women. It is the privileged few, who profit from controlling the means of production, thus appearing immune to the sickness and diseases of capitalist economies.

Answers:

1 A = Social Democratic   B = Socialist
2 A = Neoliberal   B = Social Democratic
3 A = Neoliberal   B = Socialist

Chapter summary

The chapter has signposted some of the key concepts associated with principal political ideologies. It has demonstrated that a highly polarised political analysis is not particularly beneficial, given the blurred boundaries between core values, policy-making and a fast-moving global economy. The historically determined notions of left wing, right wing and centre ground have also become muddied by a general shift to a prevailing neoliberal norm, thus marking a realignment of centre-ground politics to the right alongside the apparent demise of Communist perspectives.

As Hunter and Marks (2005) note, the drive for apolitical and pragmatic health and social care solutions has not met with universal approval, as front-line staff expect political leadership and vision rather than increased target-setting. The influence of globalisation upon the mindsets of policy-makers has also mediated a shift towards a social justice model of service provision; effectively dominated by means-tested mechanisms that are underpinned by notions of individual rights and societal responsibilities. This follows Giddens (1998) notions of 'Third Way' politics; being neither the collectivist and fully nationalised socialist infrastructure of 1970s, nor the selfish brand of deregulated libertarian individualism characterised by a Thatcherite social infrastructure a decade later. This 'Third Sector' as it is increasingly called, is a place in which the rhetoric of the 'active consumer' prevails; exerting individual choice and influence over their own health and lifestyle whilst it enabled them to make decisions over where and when they access health and social services. However, this all occurs within some state-sanctioned behaviours and rewards; consumers need to earn the right to make appropriate choices that are acceptable to both the individual and the wider community.

The final section of this chapter has considered some of the ways in which the effective practitioner can use political tools to critique both the policy and practice of contemporary health and social care. The contrasting political explanations for various health and social care issues highlight how differing political perspectives can be used to build competing 'truths'. Apolitical approaches to a health and social care context cannot claim to occupy neutral territory or to hold real validity: as illustrated, the notion of pursuing objective policy-making, grounded solely in pragmatism, is both a politically motivated gesture and highly contextual within a dominant neoliberal ideology.

Sources of further reading and exploration

Books

Barry, N. (2000) *Introduction to Modern Political Theory*. Basingstoke: Palgrave Macmillan.

Callinicos, A. T. (2001) *Against the Third Way*. Cambridge: Polity Press.

Fukuyama, F. (2006) *After the Neocons: Where the Right Went Wrong*. London: Profile Books Ltd.

Heywood, A. (2003) *Political Ideologies: An Introduction* (3rd edition). Basingstoke: Palgrave Macmillan.

MacEwan, A. (1999) *Neo-liberalism or Democracy? Economic Strategy, Markets and Alternatives for the 21st Century*. London: Zed Books.

Web

Adam Smith Institute: Right-wing think tank concerned primarily with the promotion of free market economics. Available at: www.adamsmith.org

Catalyst: Independent left-wing think tank underpinned by democratic socialism. Available at: www.catalystforum.org.uk

Demos: Centre-ground think tank for 'everyday democracy' with social justice underpinnings. Available at: www.demos.co.uk

Etzioni: Website of Amitai Etzioni, the leading thinker of Communitarianist philosophy. Available at: http://amitaietzioni.org/

Institute for Public Policy Research (IPPR): Centre–left think tank concerned with providing innovative policy solutions. Available at: www.ippr.org

Politeia: provides a forum for economic and social policy thinking about daily life, underpinned by neoliberalism. Available at: www.politeia.co.uk

Spiked: irreverent online publication concerned with 'liberty, enlightenment, experimentation and excellence'. Available at: www.spiked-online.com

6

MORAL REASONING

Liz Smith and Stella Jones-Devitt

This chapter explores applied or practical ethics and discusses the use of moral reasoning as a critical thinking tool within health and social care. It considers key ethical theories and moral principles and their application to ethical decision-making in health and social care and offers an analysis of moral reasoning as a critical thinking tool. Activities and exercises are designed to assist with the application of theory to practice and identify the link between moral reasoning and decision-making at a clinical, management and organisational level.

Chapter aims

- To explore the concept of moral reasoning as a means of critical thinking in health and social care
- To promote reflection on the relevance and value of moral reasoning to health and social care

Learning outcomes

After studying this chapter, you should be able to:

- identify the key ethical theories which underpin moral reasoning
- critically discuss contemporary issues in health and social care using moral reasoning
- evaluate the use of moral reasoning as a critical thinking tool in the context of health and social care

Key ethical theories

Many people view ethics as being purely subjective and moral values as being about personal feelings. It is certainly true that there is a tendency for all of us when faced with an ethical dilemma to respond intuitively and emotively as many of the issues which would be defined as being an ethical dilemma by their very nature tend to elicit an emotional response. Think, for instance, of the sight of starving children on the television news and it is difficult not to take a moral stance based on emotion that it is 'wrong' for countries and their politicians to focus their energies and money on civil war rather than feeding children. However, whilst the subjective response may not be wrong in itself, it is important to critically analyse why we have come to this moral judgement, as appealing merely to intuition or conscience can represent something of an easier option particularly if we are considering our own actions and decisions. Moral reasoning therefore is a means of applying ethics to a situation to attempt to ensure that the decision arrived at can be accounted for in a rational manner. Moral reasoning encourages the individual to consider any situation from all sides with an open mind rather than be judgemental. This clearly has close links with health and social care where accountability and non-judgmental decision-making are essential elements of practice. Moral reasoning can be considered to be a part of the wider sphere of applied or practical ethics.

The term 'applied ethics' has relatively recent origins having come into being in the 1970s when philosophers and academics began addressing moral problems in society and professional ethics became more prominent (Beauchamp, 2003). Whilst the origins of applied ethics are within philosophy and traditional ethical theories are relevant the focus is on addressing emerging moral problems in society. The concept of applied ethics has particular resonance with health and social care where medical ethics or bioethics is a significant area of interest and professional ethics has an impact on care delivery and policy.

There are two broad schools of normative ethical theory: utilitarianism and deontology. This section will provide a summary of the main points of these and offer some discussion of how they may be applied within the context of moral reasoning.

Utilitarianism argues that moral action is that which produces the best consequences or outcomes and is therefore sometimes referred to as conse-quentialism. When faced with a decision a person should consider the moral consequences of each of the alternatives and select the one which has the best outcome for all concerned. The 'end' for utilitarians can justify the 'means'. It focuses more on the consequences of actions and less on the actions themselves. It generates an obligation for us to do our best to increase happiness and diminish suffering so as to gain overall benefit for everybody concerned. This is an appealing theory since it is difficult to deny that best outcome is a good thing to aim for particular within the realms of health and social care where the workforce generally see the services as being of benefit to society. However it is not without its flaws. One issue which is problematic with utilitarianism is that how do we know when something is 'good' or beneficial? Perceptions of this differ greatly, particularly in relation to health. A devout Jehovah's Witness may wish to die rather than have a blood transfusion to save him, a cancer patient may prefer a shorter lifespan without the complications of treatment rather than a longer lifespan with less quality or a woman may choose a termination rather than continue with pregnancy. For some people these would be choices they would not ever consider making but for others they would seem quite appropriate.

Health and social care practitioners are often accused as being paternalistic and taking the approach that they 'know best' in determining treatment options (Jackson, 2006) and a utilitarian view of ethics in some ways encourages this as what practitioners often think is 'best' is the view that would be shared by the majority of people. This is also in line with the notion of evidence based practice as this encourages the use of treatments and interventions shown to be effective often only from a quantitative perspective rather than whether patients/clients find it beneficial in a broader more qualitative sense. This also raises another flaw in the utilitarian approach to moral action. It does not account for the needs of the minority. This is an issue which when viewed 'in theory' may not seem problematic as it can seem quite logical to go with the majority benefit, however, in practice it is not always this straightforward. Consider, for instance, the patient/client with a rare disease for whom treatment is not readily available as services are determined on health-needs analysis of the whole community. Many may still take the utilitarian approach until perhaps the patient/client in question was a relative or friend or perhaps a child then it is less easy to argue for the benefit of the majority at the cost of the few.

Campbell, Gillett and Jones (2005) offer the Christians and lions analogy in criticism of utilitarianism, if a blood thirsty majority of the population gain enjoyment from seeing the minority group of Christians being thrown to the lions does this make doing so morally right? Clearly it does not. This does underline to difficulties with utilitarianism as a single approach to deciding on moral behaviour but that does not mean that considering the consequences of a decision or action is in itself inappropriate, indeed it could be argued that means and ends are not morally separable. Whilst this analogy can be seen as problematic as it relates to a short term goal rather than a long term outcome however often health and social care seems to be about the short term as practitioners at all levels struggle with what appears to be 'crisis' management rather than long-term planning.

Deontology relates to what is absolutely right or wrong (Tschudin, 2003) and comes from the Greek 'for what is due'. Deontology is based on an unconditional respect for persons and may require doing what is right regardless of the consequences. The best known advocate of deontology is Immanuel Kant (1724–1804). The emphasis is not on the action but on the person carrying out the action and their sense of duty. Right action is determined by a set of moral rules or imperatives. This theory of ethics is closely linked with religion as a set of 'rules' that is a part of the beliefs associated with a particular religion, for example, Christians use the Ten Commandments as a basis for their moral rules. Kant believed that rules are categorical, that is that they are always applicable irrespective of want or desire. The argument to support this is that if something is deemed wrong from a rational perspective it should always be wrong and cannot be made right because we are in a different situation. Kant offers several arguments in support of this but one particular such discussion is perhaps useful to illustrate his point. Kant considered lying to be wrong as he believed it is 'the obliteration of one's dignity as a human being'. He argued that if lying was not always a wrong then we would reach a state where no-one would know if the truth were being told or not and therefore no-one would be believed. This argument is a strong one as successful lying relies on the assumption that we generally tell the truth and therefore if this assumption cannot be relied upon then lying becomes self defeating and no-one knows what the truth is.

However this approach to moral behaviour is not without its problems either. Consider a situation where you deal with a victim of serious domestic violence and her two young children who are placed in a 'safe house' for their own protection, the abusing husband then asks you where his family are. Would you tell him or would you lie? In this type of situation there is a strong argument for lying as the consequences of telling the truth could be serious for both the family and others also using the refuge, there would seem to be no moral argument for informing this violent man where his family are yet with a moral imperative lying would be wrong even in this situation. However despite these difficulties the concept of absolute rules is a strong element of health care ethics as demonstrated within codes of conduct for health professionals. Indeed there is a prevailing societal view that health care professionals who are not perceived to do their 'duty' are somehow worse morally than a lay person because of their position of trust. The idea of duty and rules to provide a framework for moral behaviour is a congenial one for some as it requires little decision-making but is perhaps in itself as much as an easy option as utilitarianism as consideration is given only to the action and not the consequences. The respect for persons may be demonstrated in the rationale for the rule but perhaps not in the individual situation as the latter is rarely 'black and white' but fraught with complexity. An alternative response to the scenario above may be to refuse to lie but to claim the overriding need to maintain confidentiality. This option stays within the principles of duty but can be seen as the less comfortable option as it requires thought and consideration of how rules can be applied constructively. However as with the notion of benefits in utilitarianism; what may be a right for one person may not be for another in terms of rules governing actions.

One issue that utilitarianism and deontology have in common as they relate to the action taken; virtue ethics however judges the character of the person committing the act and therefore arguably offers an alternative view of ethics. Whereas Kantian ethicists ask 'what should I do?' virtue ethicists ask 'what kind of person should I be?' Virtue ethics suggests that morality cannot be judged on action alone as this does not account for the morality of the motivation behind the action. Virtue ethics is applicable to health and social care and to moral reasoning in as much as it makes the practitioner think about why they want to carry out an intervention. All too often practitioners get carried away with what they want rather than caring for the patient/client and their needs. A practitioner of good character will always put the patient/client first and acknowledge their wishes and desires.

Contemporary issues in health and social care

In health and social care it is often utilitarianism which appears to govern policy as by its nature policy seeks to meet the needs of the majority. This can be seen in respect of target setting for issues such as waiting times and health promotion targets which are aimed at the major health problems of the nation. Utilitarianism can also be seen within management of health and social care services which are organised to meet the needs of the majority and not necessarily the minority. Within workforce management issues such as shift co-ordination and organisation of professional development programmes can be organised from a utilitarian perspective. Clinical care can also be delivered in such a way as to appear congruent with this perspective. Nonetheless it can also be argued that these examples can also be equally congruent with deontology in some respects. Targets are about delivering quality care, shift co-ordination is aimed at maximising skill mix to ensure good quality care – quality is clearly a duty within health and social care. The very complexity of health and social care makes it difficult at times to separate utility from duty, action from consequence.

The best known moral principles in medical or health care ethics are those suggested by Beauchamp and Childress in their book Principles of Biomedical Ethics (2001). These principles originally arose from the Belmont Report (1981) published in the USA in relation to medical research ethics. This report stated that respect for persons, beneficence and justice should be the principles that guided research. Beauchamp and Childress added non-malificence (do no harm) and these four became the cornerstone of ethics for many health and social care practitioners. The four principles to be considered according to Beauchamp and Childress are:

- respect for Autonomy
- beneficence
- non-malificence
- justice

Respect for autonomy is arguably more specific than respect for persons as this relates to the right to be 'self governing' or to make decisions for oneself. The issue then is the right of the individual patient/client to decide for themselves what they want in relation to their health care. This right is enshrined in the law on consent for health and social care however the problem here is that both the law and the principle require the individual to be deemed competent to consent or decide for themselves. This is a source of debate as defining competence is complex particularly if the decision made seems irrational. Autonomy requires the individual to decide freely and independently and the role of the practitioner is to provide appropriate information to allow informed choice. Respecting autonomy is easy when the choice made by the patient/client is what the practitioner would wish them to choose but less easy when they decide on a course of action which seems inappropriate or causes conflict in relation to the principles of beneficence and non-malificence.

Consider the case of Miss B who when realising that she was paralysed from the neck down and dependent on a ventilator for the rest of her life decided that she wanted to refuse treatment that is have the ventilator switched off. Doctors felt that this request was so irrational that they went to court to try and prove that Miss B was not competent to consent (or in this case refuse) on the basis that no 'right' minded person would choose death over life. The courts ruled that Miss B was making a rational decision, that she understood perfectly what she was asking and knew refusal of treatment would mean her death. For some this may seem to be an irrational use of autonomy but the principle behind respect for autonomy is that the individual should have their decision respected provided that they are making that decision on the basis of understanding the information given and the consequences of their actions.

Miss B chose death rather than face dependence and severely impaired quality of life. Decisions such as this can be difficult to accept in an environment whose main function is the preservation and restoration of life and health. The alternative, however, is that professionals make decisions for patients/clients and their view of what is in the 'best interests' may not be what they would want for themselves. Gillon (2003) argues that respect for autonomy should be 'first among equals' in relation to medical ethics as it is a necessary component of aspects of the other three that is beneficence, non-malificence and justice. It could also be argued that as this principle is so clearly enshrined within the law Gillon may not be alone in this viewpoint.

Activity

Think of a situation which highlights a difficulty for you as a practitioner to accept a patient/client's autonomy.

- Why did you have difficulty with it?

Beneficence is the principle of 'doing good' and involves doing what is best for patients/clients. In modern health and social care this is closely linked to the concepts of evidence based practice and clinical effectiveness. These concepts however do not always take into account what the patient/client may think is what is 'best'. Hence Gillon's (2003) claim that autonomy is so closely linked to this principle; it is the autonomous patient/client who decides what is in their best interest. Difficulties may arise in the case of the patient/client who has impaired autonomy through illness or age (as in children). Who then decides what is best for the patient? The law clearly lays responsibility for this with the clinicians in the case of an adult and generally accepts that it is the parents in the case of children. It is, however, not always easy to determine what is best for another. Take Miss B for instance, had she been unconscious she would have been unable to communicate her desire for the artificial respiration to be discontinued and it is unlikely given their stance that her clinicians would have decided this was best for her in their view.

It is possible to determine what would be the best course of action in most cases by means of evidence based practice and clinical effectiveness but neither really help in ascertaining what is best for the patient who is unable to exercise their autonomy and decide for themselves. Nonetheless from an ethical perspective the principle of beneficence holds that practitioners should make every possible effort to ensure that care is of substantial benefit to the patient/client as an individual.

Activity

Mrs Jones is 91 years old. She has mild dementia but has always managed at home with her husband. Mr Jones has to have an operation which will keep him in hospital for several days and he is worried that his wife will have an accident while he is away. Mrs Jones however does not wish to go into a local residential home for the duration as she is frightened she will never return home.

- What do you think is in the 'best interests' of the couple?

Non-malificence is the principle of 'doing no harm'. It is viewed as prima-facie duty that no harm is done to anyone whereas it can be argued that beneficence is owed to a limited number of people (Hope, 2004) as with doing good it is not always a straightforward exercise to determine what each individual would define as harm. Miss B clearly felt harm was continuing her artificial ventilation and prolonging a life of being paralysed from the neck down, her doctors however felt that harm was in letting her die.

Activity

Jon is 17 years old and has Down's Syndrome. His parents allow him very little independence but he has expressed a desire to participate in a scheme to gain employment like his friends. His parents argue that he is vulnerable to chest infections and that working would subject him to undue risk.

- What do you think will cause Jon the most harm and why?
- Should Jon be allowed to decide for himself or not?

Justice is the principle of universal fairness. It requires that all individuals have equal opportunity and that people are treated as an end in themselves not as a means to an end. It is strongly associated with anti-discriminatory and anti-oppressive practice. It is also sometimes known as the principle of universality as it holds that whatever rule of action a person has it should be capable of being universally applied to all people. It can be argued that there is a tension between individual rights and the principle of justice however the principle merely holds that there should be equal opportunity and therefore an autonomous person can accept or refuse that opportunity. Miss B was offered the opportunity, as would anyone in those circumstances, of long term care to meet her needs, however she chose to refuse.

It is argued that these four principles are the mainstay of health care ethics (Beauchamp and Childress, 2001; Beauchamp, 2003; Gillon, 2003; Macklin, 2003) and it is certainly clear that they are congruent with the underpinning philosophy of health and social care and that the case of Miss B, for example, demonstrates their applicability to practice-based dilemmas. They can also be linked to concepts such as evidence-based practice, clinical effectiveness and accountability at all levels of health and social care. They are principles that can be obviously applied to clinical care but can also be linked with management and organisational decision-making and in particular to policy-making within health and social care.

Morality, and therefore ethics, can be viewed as a subjective and even emotional rather than intellectual and reasoned. This viewpoint was held by some philosophers, for example, David Hume who held that moral judgment was primarily a matter of 'passions' (Benn, 1998). Hume, however, also sought to explore the concept of moral reasoning as he noted a logical barrier in simply arguing for moral action on the basis of a descriptive or potentially subjective claim. Hume remained convinced nonetheless that reason is subsidiary to moral deliberation. This can lead to an argument that there are no 'rights and wrongs' in ethics as each individual will hold their own view. To a certain extent this is true however it is also appropriate that to suggest that there should be some reasoned argument for a particular moral stance, it is insufficient to simply state that something is right, or wrong, without presenting some justification for it.

Moral reasoning does not necessarily mean that intuition and subjectivity have no place in the derivation of a moral stance, but it does encourage exploration of the rationale for the belief that an action is right or wrong. This is particularly true in health and social care where the moral beliefs of a practitioner or policy maker can significantly impact on others. We may not all believe the same thing about an issue but it is important to be able to account for our beliefs on issues such as abortion, euthanasia and stem cell research. This also true of more 'day-to-day' issues in health and social care which can in many ways have a more direct impact on patients and clients. Decision-making involves choice and often deciding which option to select can involve conflicting inclination, desires and interests. This conflict can simply be about issues which affect the person making the decision only and have no impact on others. However many choices can have an effect on other people and this effect may be beneficial or harmful. Where decisions do affect others then it is appropriate to consider the morality of our choices. Moral reasoning is therefore fundamentally about exploring the moral issues within a situation in order to determine what the 'best' action is and being able to offer an explanation of the reasoning behind the action.

Clinical decision-making is central to health and social care practice and therefore moral reasoning can be utilised to assist in the process of coming to a decision about the overall management of care. Moral reasoning links closely with the notion of holistic, individualised care as it encourages the practitioner to consider what is 'right' for the patient/client. Equally it is useful to consider moral reasoning within management or strategic decision-making as these decisions will have an impact on both patients/client and staff involved in delivering care, and possibly also the public at large.

In order to utilise moral reasoning as a critical thinking tool the emphasis is on rationality in ethical decision-making, the use of moral theory in problem-solving. The difficulties lie in how moral theory is used in this context. There is a school of thought which suggests that a moral rule is absolute that is if it is true in one situation it is also true in another. Therefore, if it is deemed wrong to kill another person then it is always wrong to kill irrespective of the circumstances or culture. Absolute rules are very much a part of a deontological approach to ethics. This approach may seem reasonable however it can become problematic. For example if there is an absolute rule against lying (as Kant believed) then this would mean that all lies are wrong in any circumstance including, presumably, therefore telling your child that there is a Father Christmas or a Tooth Fairy. In relation to health and social care such an absolute rule may involve truth-telling about prognosis even if it is believed to be of limited benefit to the patient. This notion of absolutism does however link with a legal view of what is right and wrong and in health and social care can be seen in the setting out of policy both at national and local level.

The alternative to absolutism could be to endorse cultural relativism that is different cultures have different moral codes and there is no universality in morality. Again this can be an apparently plausible idea. The problem arises here that it reduces morality to a matter of largely subjective opinion. It may therefore be acceptable for China to have a one-baby policy which actively advocates abortion and abandonment of babies even though it would not be acceptable in the UK. This type of argument is, however, rather simplistic and takes the idea of 'when in Rome do as the Romans do' a little too far. Can it ever be right to abandon a baby so that it starves to death in any circumstance? Is a cultural stance sufficient to justify such an action morally? It may be believed in China that the population problem can only be solved by a stringent law on the size of a family, it may also be believed that male children are of more value to the family than girls but does that make it 'right' to abandon a female child in order to try for a boy? This is perhaps an extreme, although real example, but it highlights the difficulties of basing morality on belief alone.

Rachels (1999) makes the point that some people believed the earth was flat, whilst some believed it was spherical but this did not mean there was no objective truth in geography. Whilst ethics cannot be as objective and empirical as subjects such as geography it is no less acceptable to maintain an argument based purely on subjective and descriptive belief. In health and social care cultural norms must have their place in decision-making about individuals but this should be based on the autonomous and informed choices rather than a belief that 'anything is right if you justify it' in relation to a cultural belief.

An alternative to either absolutism or relativism in health and social care could be moral sensitivity. Jaeger (2001, p. 139) describes moral sensitivity as 'openness to the differences that can exist between people involved in a particular decision-making situation and depends on both an understanding and respect for the complexity of meaningfulness in human life'. This would seem in some ways to provide some middle ground between the notions of absolutism and relativism and be in keeping with the fact that no two health and social care situations are identical. It links closely with the feminist ethic of caring which places value on feelings, desires and the constraints of the people involved in a decision-making situation. It allows that absolute rules may not always be possible but also does not simply accept that moral action cannot be determined by subjective belief only; there needs to be some consideration of each situation which involves an element of empathy as well as the application of theoretical principles.

Activity

Consider the following situations from a position of absolutism and then from cultural relativism.

1   Abortion
2   Euthanasia

- What, if any, are the differences in the way these issues would be addressed?
- Does one approach appeal to you more than the other, if so, why?

Mary is a 56-year-old teacher who has been diagnosed with a terminal disease which will gradually make her unable to communicate in the latter stages. She does not wish her carers to attempt resuscitation of any sort at any stage of her disease and has written an advance directive to support this wish.

Joe is 73 years old and has suffered a myocardial infarction. He has an active and independent life normally and is the main carer for his disabled wife. Both these patients collapse.

- Should they be resuscitated?
- Are your decisions for each different? If so, why is this do you think?
- Do you think your decisions reflect moral sensitivity?

Moral reasoning as a critical thinking tool in health and social care

There are models and frameworks offered to aid ethical decision-making within much of the literature (Thompson, Melia and Boyd, 2000; Tschudin, 2003 for example). These models and frameworks have their merits however they also have limitations depending on the situation relating to the decision. There are some basic principles which arguably can be applied to most situations.

- Define the problem: This is a basic step which should start any decision-making process but has importance in ethical decision-making because it is often easy to be subjective and judgmental about a situation where only limited information is gained and therefore understanding is lacking. This process of defining the problem allows the decision maker to frame the issues in context with the situation. It can aid with moral sensitivity as well as with the reasoning process. Points to consider here are the facts of the situation or problem, identify those involved, what is the main ethical problem therefore to be addressed. From a moral reasoning perspective this first step is essential as it encourages a more reasoned approach to an ethical decision.
- Determine the ethical theory or principles which are relevant to the problem: It may be an organisational problem which requires the broader sweep of the main normative theories or a more individualised problem which lends itself to the four moral principles offered by Beauchamp and Childress (2001). That is not to suggest that normative theories cannot be applied to individuals or the four principles to organisational issues but that it is appropriate to utilise a theoretical approach which has relevance to the main ethical problem identified.
- Analyse the options: The possible options for action need to be analysed in relation to the theoretical approach and a moral course of action selected.
- Evaluation of the outcome: Feedback should be gained in relation to the moral goals. This feedback will aid the decision maker to reflect on the process and outcome and thereby assist with future ethical decision-making.

The steps outlined above can be applied to a clinical, management or organisational problem. In the case of Miss B the problem is quite easy to define and the four principles can be applied as discussed above to arrive at a decision regarding discontinuance of her treatment. The difficulty may seem to be here the gaining of feedback however Miss B would communicate her compliance with the switching-off process or indicate a desire to change her mind. In a management or organisational context it is often useful to consider the ethical dimension of a problem to ensure compliance with corporate governance, and in health and social care this is particularly true since it is a public service and one which needs to ensure that its decisions take into account public opinion and expectations as well as legal requirements such as Equal Opportunities and Health and Safety. Criticism is often made in relation to such measures as cost effectiveness, target setting and policy-making, however these are not unethical concepts in themselves but the decision-making processes do not involve consideration of moral issues and therefore the result may appear lacking in morality or concern for those affected. Policy can actually be supportive of a more ethical approach, for example public and service user involvement in services and developments. Processes such as stakeholder analysis can encourage consideration of the four principles and how they may be applied to the identified stakeholders.

It has been shown above that there are limitations to ethical theories and principles to fully address the complexity of health and social care issues; however, this can be addressed by an eclectic approach to ethical decision-making. Utilitarian approaches to service delivery can be tempered by consideration of justice, deontology can be linked with beneficence and non-malificence to ensure that some consideration of outcome is made.

Activity

Consider the following four problems using the principles for ethical decision-making outlined above.

1   Mr A has a long-term illness which has now deteriorated to the point where little can be done other than ensure his symptoms are controlled as much as possible to maintain a degree of comfort for him. He is unaware of his poor prognosis and his family wish him to remain so as they believe he will 'give in'.

  • Should Mr A be told or not?

2   Len is 50 years old and an alcoholic. He has just been discharged from hospital for complications arising from his alcohol problem. He lives in a top floor flat and, as his social worker; you are concerned for his safety. His friends echo your concerns however Len is adamant he wants to be left alone and does not want any sort of intervention.

  • What are your options?

3   You manage a respite care for the elderly service which is currently not meeting the needs of its clients as there is not enough staff to maintain safe levels of care delivery. You are given the following options to address this: the service can be discontinued altogether and staff deployed to support other more acute services for the elderly or you can reduce the service to keep the beds open Monday to Friday.

  • Which option should you select on an ethical basis?

4   The local area has been granted government funds to expand acute hospital services. These funds can be used to extend an existing city hospital to create a 'centre of excellence' for critical care provision for adults and children or they can be used to build a new hospital delivering general medicine and surgery and outpatients facilities to the neighbouring market town and surrounding rural area.

  • Which option do you think is the most ethical choice?

(Continued)

(Continued)

Consider whether your reasoned decision was any different from your initial intuitive reaction to each scenario.

- Were there any issues which you had not thought of until you analysed the scenarios in the light of ethical theory?

Chapter summary

Moral reasoning encourages a rational and intellectual approach to decision-making which allows the individual to be able to offer an ethical argument for their chosen stance. The consideration of the problem from a reasoned rather than intuitive perspective facilitates a more considered view of right and wrong. This does not mean that individuals will necessarily reach the same conclusions as others but it does mean that their viewpoint can be accounted for. This is entirely in keeping with the notion of critical thinking which encourages intellectual inquiry and open-mindedness.

Health and social care involves practitioners and managers in many situations which have an ethical element within them and it is important that critical thinking in relation to both clinical care and service delivery encompasses moral reasoning. This will ensure that health and social care delivery is in keeping with accountability and effectiveness and also with a philosophy of a service for the public whether this is publicly or privately funded. Moral reasoning is congruent with both individualised and holistic approach to care management and also with corporate governance and ethical management within health and social care services. This approach to critical thinking therefore is a practical aid to decision-making at all levels within health and social care.

Sources of further reading and exploration

Books

Almond, B. (1998) *Exploring Ethics: A Traveller's Tale*. Oxford: Blackwell.

Banks, S. (2004) *Ethics, Accountability and the Social Professions*. Basingstoke: Palgrave Macmillan.

Hugman, R. (2005) *New Approaches in Ethics for the Caring Professions*. Basingstoke: Palgrave Macmillan.

Thomson, A. (1999) *Critical Reasoning in Ethics: A Practical Introduction*. London: Routledge.

White, J. E. (2000) *Contemporary Moral Problems*. (6th edition). Belmont, CA: Wadsworth Publishing Company.

For the court report re Miss B
www.hmcourts-service.gov.uk/judgmentsfiles/j1075/BvNHS.htm
http://plato.stanford.edu/entries/reasoning-moral/
http://en.wikipedia.org/wiki/Moral_reasoning
http://info.nwmissouri.edu/~rfield/274guide/274overview2.htm

7

FEMINISM AND POST-FEMINISM

Stella Jones-Devitt and Julie Dickinson

This chapter considers some of the many perspectives and debates around contemporary views of feminism. It provides an overview of key ideas, starting from an examination of early historical developments underpinning the social construction of women to more specific notions identified under the rubric of 'Feminism' per se. The chapter covers three main strands of feminist theory, encompassing radical feminism, socialist feminism and post-feminism. It does not attempt to embrace all the divergent viewpoints within the limitations of the chapter length, but captures the overarching themes that prevail in order to provide some critical perspectives in relation to health and social care.

Chapter aims

- To provide an overview of key ideas associated with feminism and post-feminism
- To promote refection upon the relevance and value of feminist and post-feminist theories to the context of health and social care

Learning outcomes

After studying this chapter, you should be able to:

- identify key concepts associated with feminism and post-feminism
- critically analyse similarities and differences between feminist and post-feminist theories
- critically discuss contemporary issues in health and social care using feminist and post-feminist theories

Key concepts associated with feminism and post-feminism

The term 'feminism' is highly contested with a plethora of perspectives holding some very different conceptual bases. Opinions vary as to whether 'feminism' per se, still exists, or whether society has entered a Post-Feminist phase, in which male–female tensions are inconsequential. This chapter highlights three of the key theories influencing debates around feminism. The chosen theories range from the essentialist notions of radical feminism, in which differences between men and women are taken as fixed, irreconcilable and desirable; socialist feminism, that views gender as only one facet of oppression amongst many others; post-feminism, in which an apolitical stance prevails, suggesting that the supposed war of the sexes is unnecessary, spurious and vacuous. In addition to macro-Feminist theories, the 'F' word itself evokes a broad range of commentaries from many different sources, underpinned by many contrasting views.

US Republican politician, Pat Robertson (1992) offers an unsophisticated one-size-fits-all notion of feminism, resulting in a damning indictment of the feminist movement, which he describes as: 'a socialist, anti-family movement that encourages women to leave their husbands, kill their children, practice witchcraft, destroy capitalism and become lesbians' (cited in Siann, 1994, p. 125). A different view, yet arguably one lacking equally in sophistication, is offered by US actress, Roseanne Barr (1993) who believes that all women should apply her unique type of Post-feminist logic: 'The thing women have got to learn is that nobody gives you power, you just take it' (cited in Siann, 1994, p. 125).

In contrast to the above two views, Germaine Greer, once lauded as a key spokeswoman for the Feminist agenda, suggests that in the twenty first century, Feminist issues have become subtler with more insidious forms of oppression occurring. Greer (1999) notes that:

> The person is still political. The Millennial feminist has to be aware that oppression exerts itself in and through her most intimate relationships, beginning with the most intimate, her relationship with her body. More and more of her waking hours are to be spent in disciplining the recalcitrant body, fending off the diseases that it is heir to and making up for its inadequacies in size, shape weight, colouring, hair distribution, muscle tone and orgiastic efficiency, and its incorrigible propensity for ageing. (p. 329)

Whatever the analysis, Feminist perspectives focus on two main premises concerning:

1 the extent to which men's domination has resulted in subordination of women in society
2 whether this domination (intended or otherwise) has created a framework of 'patriarchy' in which men's achievements are valued higher than women's

Until the recent appearance of post-feminism, these aspects were analysed from either an essentialist or structuralist global view. Siann (1994) explains that essentialism locates patriarchy within fundamental biological and physiological differences between women and men; it does not accept that male–female differences are mediated primarily by social and cultural conditioning. The roots of essentialism can be traced far back to Ancient Greece, in which ideas of a fixed natural order in society were believed. Such order was determined by physical differences between the sexes, with males providing the superior form whilst women provided the inferior matter. This resulted in a conceptualisation of dualisms, upon which much of the later assumptions around the sexes were based.

The fixed nature idea also led to the instigation of amoral social hierarchies; thus, as relations between men and women were so immutable, there was no value in doing anything other than accepting one's fate. This was clearly more beneficial to males as they were thought to be of higher biological worth than females, whom were ascribed the role of vessel carrier of the future generations. Throughout early Christianity and until the Renaissance period, an explicit objectification of the female body continued. Examples abound: the Christian tale of Adam and Eve mirrors an essentialist slant, viewing women as moral wreckers whose primary purpose and use-value was in relation to fertility. Certain female physiological processes were viewed pejoratively; for example, the representation of menstruation has been given an evil significance as it goes against the intention of reproduction, signifying physical breakdown and failure to conceive.

Essentialist concepts continued to gain credibility throughout the Middle Ages until well into the nineteenth century, in which the obsession with exploring human 'nature' and trait categorization developed into a set of binary opposites; hence, if men were rational, women were irrational, if men were strong, women were weak. The key notion underpinning later binary analyses related to beliefs that it was evolutionary, productive to have separate female and male ways of thinking. Application of a binary idyll was prevalent in many of the emerging disciplines and professions of the time; hence, the strong links to medicine, psychology and biology, manifested by Darwinism and eugenics alongside evolutionary psychology and socio-biology.

The Radical Feminist perspective is grounded firmly in essentialist notions of difference; however, radical feminists do not accept that the explicit differences ascribed to females are inferior, rather the opposite view that essentially female traits need redefining and revaluing positively. Jones (1996) asserts that radical feminism begins with the premise: 'the person is political, radical feminists argue that to adopt traditional political methods would be to play into the hands of male institutions. They seek instead to recreate their own world, their own reality, and give energy to new, female-centered institutions rather than the old male ones' (p. 34).

Activity

Consider the notion that men and women are essentially different.

- Do you think that this is a valid viewpoint?
- Does this viewpoint have any influence on your practice?

In contrast, structuralist approaches view male–female relations to be highly dependent on socio-cultural conditions and processes. Siann (1994) describes how structuralism emerged primarily from the late nineteenth century onwards, encompassing a wide range of perspectives and analyses, including:

- Feminist psychology, linked to structuralism through social learning theory and its role in shaping sex-typed behaviour, in direct opposition to much early psychoanalytical reasoning
- Existentialism, propounded by Sartre and De Beauvoir during the 1950s, with its principal idea that humans are self-creating individuals who make choices through life, not by being predisposed to particular psychological traits
- Constructionism, a late twentieth-century perspective evolving from early nineteenth-century feminist psychology, yet updated to recognise that much contemporary psychological reasoning is discussed from within a white middle-class, male-privileged approach
- Postmodernism, which claims that there are no absolute or universal truths, yet acknowledges that female–male relations are affected by the particular bias of cultural location

Socialist feminism is one of the major ideas explored within this chapter that epitomises a structural approach. As Ehrenreich (2005) notes, it views gender as only one facet of oppression, explaining that the working classes in any capitalist society will be disadvantaged and sub-divided purposefully; hence, the reason why male–female relations are economically determined and engineered to be fractious. The viewing of male–female relations through an economic imperative is in stark contrast to the Radical Feminist agenda. The founding statement of the New York Radical Feminists (1969) offers a very different view to the above assertions, claiming that economic issues have little to do with female oppression:

> We believe that the purpose of male chauvinism is primarily to obtain psychological ego satisfaction, and that only secondarily does this manifest itself in economic relationships. For this reason we do not believe that capitalism, or any other economic system, is the cause of female oppression, nor do we believe that female oppression will disappear as a result of a purely economic revolution. (Cited in Smith, 1994 p. 9)

Post-feminism originates from a US white middle-class perspective, emerging from the mid-1980s onwards. It developed from an apolitical perspective that, in early days, was manifested by 'Girl Power' and latterly by the concept of women 'having it all'. This perspective believes that all women have to do is stop playing 'victim' and to seize the opportunities now available. Post-feminism views that women can compete successfully on an equal basis as 'individuals'; this aligns it with a wider neoliberal ideology based upon pragmatism, choice, market freedom and a brand of individualism premised on anti-collectivism. Epstein (2002) notes that the rise of individualism, and the ensuing pre-occupation with work as the key source of identity for many, has removed the explicit feminist debate from the consciousness of most women. A literal interpretation of post-feminism suggests that feminism no longer exists politically or in the wider public sphere.

Whelehan (1995) suggests that this is represented clearly within media portrayal, with once-marginalised feminist pioneers such as Germaine Greer becoming regulars in mainstream television chat shows, either to be constructed as quaint relics of past revolutionary times or invited to eschew the views they once championed. Gillis and Munford (2004) suggest that this is indicative of a shift towards post-feminist representation of women within mainstream media, in which the dichotomy between 'Victim Feminism' and 'Power Feminism' is overplayed; it implies that to be liberated from victim hood, women have to celebrate taking power through their achievements in both public and private spheres, seeing female successes as 'normal' not heroic or unusual.

Historically, the development of feminist theory is described through a 'wave' analogy. 'First wave' feminists were primarily the upper-class suffragettes and female agitators fighting for votes for women and greater acceptance of women in the public domain. 'Second wave' feminism emerged in the post-World War II period of the twentieth century and spawned the Women's Liberation movement alongside emerging radical feminist and socialist feminist philosophies. As Epstein (2002) notes, this began as the preserve of university-educated, disenchanted middle-class women, yet spread to encompass the voices of ordinary working-class women through the organisation of local collective action and community engagement. Gillis and Munford (2004) imply that 'Third wave' feminism is commonly perceived to be a fusion of 'academic' post-feminist theory and non-academic approaches fuelled by the dissatisfaction with existing feminist analyses. Wolf (1993) suggests that this backlash is primarily against inaccessible academic theorising that has no relevance and significance to the lived experience of ordinary women and men.

Similarities and differences between feminist and post-feminist theories

The table below articulates some of the similarities and differences between the three selected strands of feminist analysis, covering: a general overview of each theoretical perspective; how each theory explains sources of oppression; the underpinning sexual politics; how body image and the politics of appearance impact on women; proposed solutions.

Activity

Please appraise Table 7.1 and relevant commentaries on each section. Imagine there is an additional section added, entitled 'Impact on care'.

- Consider how each perspective would justify its approach
- Which of the theories aligns most closely to your present practice?

Overview: Radical feminism locates patriarchy within the explicit differences between women and men, arguing that it is not due primarily to socio-cultural processes, but is symptomatic of the innate physiological and psychological divergence of males and females as two separate and distinct species. Socialist feminism concurs that patriarchy exists, yet views it as a by-product of a divisive capitalist ethos in which gender relations are merely one element of wider class oppression. Ehrenreich (2005) criticises the radical feminist perspective as remaining transfixed on concepts of male supremacy, resulting in a stagnant ideological impasse instead of collective action. A post-feminist analysis eschews notions of patriarchy, suggesting instead that male-led oppression is spurious as individuals have responsibility for negotiating relationships in both public and private spheres, regardless of gender.

Sources of oppression: Not a great deal of consensus between the three perspectives on this point; Jones (1996) notes that radical feminists lay the blame clearly on patriarchy, with males as both the principal instigators and beneficiaries of gendered privilege and societal advantage. Socialist feminists imply that a range of gender, race and cultural tensions is generated by the de-humanising aspects of capitalism via the alienation of its workforce for maximum productivity. They contend that patriarchy does exist, but as a tool of capitalism to fuel structural division between male and female workers. Only post-feminists ascribe any real blame to women, contending that females

Table 7.1 Feminist theories: key similarities and differences

	Radical feminism	Socialist feminism	Post-feminism
Overview	Essentialist patriarchy generates fundamental differences between men and women	Gender is only one element of wider social class oppression via a capitalist ethos that inevitably leads to male–female economic tensions and divisions	Old-fashioned feminism is dead. Women can compete equally with men on an individual basis
Main source of oppression	System of patriarchy in which all aspects of society are viewed and privileged from a male perspective	De-humanising aspects of capitalism, which seeks to sub-divide oppressed groups in order to maximise profit. Views much feminist theory as bourgeois posturing	Women themselves, who continue to enshrine outdated victim-hood based on spurious notions of gender oppression
Sexual politics	Rejects heterosexuality as it is a major tool of patriarchy. Sees heterosexual feminists as token feminists. Denies the concept of male feminists	Embraces all forms of sexuality whilst acknowledging that male–female sexual relations can be mediated by economics. Accepts that men can be feminists	Embraces all forms of sexuality as creative expressions of individuality. Rejects notions of sexual manipulation based on gendered power relations. Assumes that nobody needs to be a feminist per se
Politics of appearance	Celebrates the 'natural' state of unfettered women-hood and resists patriarchal notions of beauty. Rejects androgyny as a coping response	Views the politics of appearance as a divisive capitalist tool that obfuscates the key reasons of oppression	Rejects that the politics of appearance oppresses women specifically; indeed, welcomes the rights of all women to choose their own tools of empowerment, including the right to look good
Proposed solutions	Views separate development as central; also requires more positive revaluing of womanly differences	Requires the active consciousness-raising of all oppressed groups, via collective resistance to capitalism	Insists that traditional feminism has damaged the progress of women by making them victims; women should take responsibility for their own empowerment

have played learned helplessness tactics for far too long. They also view traditional feminist approaches as divisive, outdated and counter-productive to progress, suggesting that a feminist backlash has been fuelled by the approaches adopted by earlier radical feminists.

Sexual politics: Radical feminist theory views heterosexuality as constructed from a purely male perspective. It includes analyses of sexual violence and pornography as indicators of heterosexual patriarchy and coercion of women; even eroticism is rejected as a cultural construction of male dominance. Socialist feminism acknowledges the validity of all forms of sexuality yet accepts that male–female sexual relations are mediated by power gained from economic privilege, with many women using sexual favour as a discrete bargaining tool in the private domain. Unlike the radical feminist strand, socialist feminists accept that men can be feminists, arguing that they are also oppressed by patriarchal expectations and socially constructed to act in specific 'male' ways, useful for sustaining a capitalist infrastructure. Post-feminists contend that all forms of sexuality are essentially creative expressions of individuality, not gendered constructs per se. They reject that sexual activity is located primarily in male–female power relations; indeed, they celebrate notions of aggressive female sexual appetite as proof of women's equality and empowerment.

Politics of appearance: There is minimal consensus between the three perspectives, with each taking a contrasting position. Radical feminism welcomes a return to a 'natural' state of woman-hood, suggesting that women should resist patriarchal pressures to make themselves acceptable to the male 'gaze' by feeling comfortable with their essential female core. Post-feminists reject notions that the politics of appearance oppresses women specifically; indeed, they welcome the rights of all women as individuals, to choose how they wish to appear, arguing that such choice is empowering women rather than denying them opportunities. The socialist–feminist perspective views a focus on the politics of appearance as an unnecessary diversion that obfuscates the real issues of disempowerment; it cites alienating aspects of work and capitalist infrastructures as the major tools of oppression for both women and men.

Activity

- What is the media's defined image of an 'ideal' woman?
- Does this 'image' influence your lifestyle?
- Does media portrayal influence your practice?
- Does it influence your patients/clients expectations of the service you provide?

Proposed solutions: Yet more divergence between the three perspectives. Radical feminists believe that liberation from patriarchy requires completely separate development. They assert that women should glory in their 'womanly' difference, as Rich (1987) notes: 'I have come to believe . . . that female biology – the diffuse, intense sensuality radiating out from the clitoris, breast, uterus, vagina; the lunar cycles of menstruation; the gestation and fruition of life which can take place in the female body – has far more radical implications than we have yet come to appreciate' (cited in Segal, p. 9). This approach should lead to a positive re-valuing of qualities such as passion, fertility and irrationality; aspects that radical feminists argue are despised and trivialised by patriarchy.

Socialist feminism sees the only solution to women's oppression through the overthrow of capitalist economies. It argues that this can only be achieved through a collective response to capitalism rather than by focusing on a single issue. In contrast to a post-feminist perspective, socialist feminists view capitalist intrusion into the private domain as very damaging to women's autonomy. Ehrenreich (2005) states:

The forces which have atomized working-class life and promoted cultural/material dependence on the capitalist class are the same forces which have served to perpetuate the subjugation of women. It is women who are most isolated in what has become an increasingly privatized family existence (even when they work outside of the home too). It is, in many instances, women's skills which have been discredited or banned to make way for commodities. It is, above all, women who are encouraged to be utterly passive/uncritical/dependent (i.e. "feminine") in the face of the persuasive capitalist penetration of private life. (p. 76)

Post-feminism contends that patriarchy is dead and, whilst acknowledging the gains made by past-feminist resistance, suggests that the time is now ripe to move into new insights about the nature of social life and power relations. Becker (2000) articulates that:

One strand of Post-Feminism is the idea that feminism as a social movement, having pushed us all towards a more egalitarian society (which is now self-evidently a good thing for which we are all of course grateful) is now essentially over, and a radicalism associated with it has been appropriately replaced by approaches to gender that seek consensus and value men's experiences. (p. 399)

Application of feminist/post-feminist theories to contemporary issues in health and social care

Post-feminist views reflect some of the ascendant issues in contemporary health and social care policy and practice, mirroring the prevailing neoliberal economy that promises choice, flexibility, consumer freedom and individual rewards. Underpinning the overarching post-feminist perspective that the 'equality battle' has been achieved, health and social care policy has absorbed a gender-neutral approach; hence, 'mothers' become 'parents' in government strategy on parental leave, and 'well women' clinics now encapsulate a more embracing 'well persons' ethos. However, some gender differences still prevail. Daykin (2001) notes that the majority of women continue to live longer than men, yet paradoxically they experience a higher level of reported ill health; reasons for this fit into a post-feminist ideology as possible explanations can be ascribed to our differing biological constitutions rather than perceived discrimination. However, as Doyal (2002) asserts, social factors especially around unequal access to resources, nutrition and reproductive health, counteract this positive outcome, suggesting that structural factors do result in unequal health outcomes for women.

Second wave feminists assert that women have been subjected to on-going processes of medicalisation in determining their health status, in which the starting point is the problematic female body and its deficiencies. Both Oakley (1993) and Bordo (1995) contend that medicalisation has influenced the lived experiences of women far more than those of men. Radical feminists such as Richardson (1993) contend that the male gaze built around the objectification of the female form adds to the notion that women's bodies are things that can be 'done to', modified and controlled, as inferior physiological beings. She uses the concept of motherhood to animate the debate, arguing that its social construction assumes procreation to be the greatest feat for most women; thus failure to be a mother suggests something 'unnatural' and unfulfilled, whilst expressing dissatisfaction with the mothering process per se, is blamed upon a pre-disposition for dysfunction of mind and/or body rather than through acknowledgement of any legitimate misgivings.

Oakley (1993) notes that there is a strong emphasis on the concept of women as primary carers of other people's health, reinforcing a sense of insignificance that is defined only in relation to fulfilment of other's health. She argues that the main cause of the inequitable positioning of women in society results from unequal divisions of labour, in which women earn far less generally, hold less prestigious roles and have the reduced status that goes alongside; this gives them neither the bargaining power nor the 'earned' rights to respect in the private family domain or within health care. Oakley (1993) also asserts that much of the health care process is divided along gendered lines, with certain professions such as nursing becoming more feminised, and more trivialised. She comments:

> Some time ago, nursing was dubbed a 'semi-profession' along with others dominated by women (school teaching and social work). In fact, the predominance of women in these occupations was counted as a reason for their lack of full professional status,

women being said to be less committed to employment than men and more interested in on-the-job personal relations than in such 'masculine' attributes as long-term training programmes. (p. 49)

Despite stark evidence to the contrary by Oakley (1993) and Doyal (2002), post-feminists view that all women need to do is to learn how to empower themselves by looking good, being a good role model and showing willingness to reinvent their persona, as necessary. Kersten (1994) implies that women have had no option but to seize their opportunities in this manner, due to second wave feminists' transformation of the strong and enduring female form into what she describes as 'the empty vessel' (p. 2). She argues that the new post-feminist woman has had to emerge in the 1990s from the unhealthy victim portrayed from the 1960s onwards. She defines this woman as: 'the empty vessel of post sixties feminist theory . . . a timid, weak, and bewildered creature. She is defined by her suffering and victim hood. She lacks the internal resources to cope with suffering . . . Easily threatened, she is only comfortable operating within the context of a group, a "sisterhood" of like-minded victims' (pp. 2–3).

Gillis and Munford (2004) contend that a new, media-friendly, form of post-feminism has emerged, underpinned by the explicit distinction between 'Victim Feminism' and 'Power Feminism'. Despite this rhetoric, structural explanations show that women are still disadvantaged in both public and private spheres of life. They earn less, have lower paid jobs and undertake the bulk of unpaid caring and domestic work; powerful factors contributing to inequalities in health.

The shift in health care towards terminology around 'self-care', 'client-centeredness' 'expert patient' and 'autonomous practitioner' reflects a post-feminist, neoliberal ascendancy, where power and responsibility is placed with the client, patient or worker as an individual, dependent upon whom is seen as in the empowered position. This has resulted in the ideal of empowering self and others through the development of a range of process-based skills, including problem-solving, assertiveness and confidence-building. In a nursing context, Dalziel (2003) criticises this approach as being over-simplistic and linear, contending that nurses often talk about empowering their patients as if they own the ability to give them the power they need; mistakenly, professionals often equate giving the client access to information as a process of empowerment, rather than one of mere information exchange.

The limits of this approach are most clearly reflected when professional groups in health and social care aspire to become autonomous practitioners. This new role is championed through government policy, workforce skills quangos and professional organisations; yet Davies (2002) asserts it is of questionable merit for women in particular; especially in professions where development has been defined primarily via patriarchal workplace practices.

One of the World Health Organisation's key global health policy drivers, the Ottawa Charter (1986) describes empowerment as a mechanism that enables individuals, organisations and communities to gain mastery over their lives and to control their own health. To achieve this, egalitarian structures must be provided to ensure that all health and social care professionals, regardless of gender, have control over their own practice prior to attempting to empower anybody else (Dickinson and Jones-Devitt, 2003 and Latter, 1998).

The ascendancy of a 'self-care' ethos within the management of long-term conditions reflects the 'can do' notions of a post-feminist neoliberal ideology. This is characterised by moving away from a medically defined prevention of illness model towards a wider, more seductive concept of 'client-centred' health. This approach is engrained within individualist behaviour-change models where motivational theories are used with women in promoting outcomes such as being slim (obesity programmes), not smelling of tobacco (smoking-cessation programmes) and having a toned body (exercise programmes). Taylor (2003) asserts that this approach perpetuates the 'women to-be-looked-at-ness' exemplified by the gendered nature of the politics of appearance; yet remaining unchallenged by post-feminist theorists. Paradoxically, the additional pressure placed upon women's appearance could actually sabotage any positive effects on helping to change health-damaging behaviours, by setting out unrealistic ideals that most women cannot achieve.

Activity

Consider the following points in relation to self-care perspectives:

- In your own practice, are you encouraged to empower patients/clients?
- Think of one example in practice and consider the advantages and disadvantages

---

The socialist feminist agenda is visible in health and social care policy analyses that consider the affect of social structures and provision on women's overall wellbeing. Foster (1995) suggests that there are power and equity issues for women accessing health and social care services. She considers the notion of health promotion to articulate some of the wider debates concerning health policy and women. Foster (1995) asserts that many of the key policy drivers rely upon:

- Inaccurate health data for women
  This approach relies on figures of males-only data and applies it unreservedly to extrapolating evidence to plan whole population's health policy.

- Exerting oppressive social control over women's lives
  Women are far more likely to be medicalised, pathologised, objectified and certified more mentally ill than men. Women are targeted as holding primary responsibility for family health and for being principal carers within the private domain.
- Ignoring the primary causes of women's morbidity and quality of life
  Lack of control over one's own life is the key determinant of both quality of life and perceived morbidity. Patriarchal societies deny women equal access to education, employment, reproductive control, economic prosperity and general acceptance within the public domain.

ACTIVITY

The UK Government's health strategy 'Choosing Health: making healthy choices easier' (Department of Health, 2004) has a number of priority areas and suggested action for enhancing public health and social care services. One area is the introduction of personal health guides. This will be unique to the individual and give them the opportunity to: work out for themselves the health status of their current lifestyle; set out ambitions for their own health; determine what action they want to take and what support they can expert to get from the NHS and others in order to achieve their expressed ambitions.

- Using some or all of the feminist viewpoints discussed in this chapter, how would you target your help as a health and social care professional to support the implementation of these personal health guides?

Chapter summary

This chapter has explored some of the key concepts associated with feminism and its use as a potential tool of critical analysis. The term itself is highly contested and value laden, from views of the F word as being emancipatory and liberating, to an association with out-of-date victim-hood and dourness. Feminist debate centres around two key concerns: the global subordination of women and commonalities that underpin this experience; processes of patriarchy and the extent to which societal infrastructures need to be dismantled to fulfil women's best interests. The roots and development of essentialist explanations of male/female difference have been examined briefly, alongside the emergence of structural perspectives that seek to recognise how socially constructed gender identities influence everyday lived experiences.

Feminist theorists consider the oppression of women within both public and private spheres of existence; public forms relate to social and economic relations conducted within the wider 'visible' social infrastructure, whilst domestic and intimate familial activity occurs within the private 'invisible' sphere. Although this division has provided fertile ground for social commentators, the erosion of private into public, as characterised in the ascendancy of individualism, has led to a blurring of boundaries and a redefining of whether this distinction is still meaningful and valid for further Feminist analysis.

This chapter traces the historical objectification of women back to days of Ancient Greece and notions of the inferior woman being a vessel carrier for future male leaders. The exploration of human nature and trait categorisation gathered pace until the nineteenth century, spawning a set of binary opposites that confirmed the evolutionary separateness of male and female ways of thinking; these were applied to all kinds of emerging disciplines like medicine, psychology and biology, alongside the newer ideological approaches of Darwinism, evolutionary psychology and the Eugenics movement. Structuralist theories gained some credibility from the early twentieth century onwards, encompassing a wide range of perspectives, including: feminist psychology, existentialism, constructionism and postmodernism; all seeking to go beyond the male/female innate differences approach to uncover how social processes reinforce these purported differences and stymie opportunity.

The three 'waves' of feminist theory-building illustrate how theories are very much products of their time; from the first wave suffragettes of the early twentieth century whose primary purpose was to secure votes; the permissive 1960s in which the second wave focused on women's liberation and social upheaval; finally, the current third wave approach, characterised by the politics of the individual and their rights as active consumers rather than via any gender distinctions and collective action.

The three selected strands of Feminist theory, namely radical feminism, socialist feminism and post-feminism provide a diverse range of approaches, each offering their own explanations for sources of oppression, sexual politics, politics of appearance and perceived solutions. Radical feminism eschews social integration, offering separate development as the way forward. This is antithetical to a post-feminist perspective that suggests the abandonment of sexual politics per se, alongside a reconceptualisation away from pursuing collective social relations to ones based upon individual need and mutual negotiation. Socialist feminism spans some of this conceptual impasse, asserting that sexual politics do mediate women's experiences and therefore cannot be ignored, yet these occur within the wider context of capitalist economic drivers in which division of labour and factionalism serve a profit imperative.

Application of feminist tools of analysis in contemporary neoliberal health and social care is highlighted through articulation to several emerging themes: post-feminist alliances to self-care concepts in which the person 'empowers' him/herself in a range of health care situations; Medicalised motherhood processes that radical feminists claim are entrenched in patriarchy and oppression; socialist feminist critiques of behaviour-change approaches for promoting the public's health, in which women are often targeted primarily as arbiters of family health alongside health policy development that ignores wider structural inequalities. Changes to the professions supporting health and social care are discussed, whilst the implications of 'feminised' occupational roles are considered within the developing neoliberal economy.

Sources of further reading and exploration

Books

Bendelow, G., Carpenter, M., Vautier, C. and Williams, S. (eds) (2001) *Gender, Health and Healing: The Public/Private Divide*. London: Routledge.

Foster, P. (1995) *Women and the Health Care Industry: An Unhealthy Relationship*. Milton Keynes: Open University Press.

Greer, G. (1999) *The Whole Woman*. London: Doubleday.

Oakley, A. (1993) *Essays on Women, Medicine and Health*. Edinburgh: Edinburgh University Press.

Stein, J. (1997) *Empowerment and Women's Health: Theory, Methods and Practice*. London: Zed Books.

Ussher, J. (ed.) (2000) *Women's Health: Contemporary International Perspectives*. Oxford: Blackwell.

Web

The Fawcett Society: a campaigning organization concerned primarily with women's representation in politics and public life and with pay and poverty issues. The site has a useful library of downloadable resources. Available at: www.fawcettsociety.org.uk/

The F Word: an organization dedicated to sharing ideas about contemporary UK feminism. Available at: www.thefword.org.uk/

The Women's Library: comprehensive academic resource dedicated to recording the history of women's lives. Available at: www.thewomenslibrary.ac.uk

—— **8** ——

CRITICAL REALISM

Stella Jones-Devitt and Liz Smith

This chapter considers some of the major concepts and debates associated with critical realism. It provides an overview of key ideas underpinning critical realism and its development as a theory. The chapter covers the overarching themes that prevail, assisting the reader through specific exercises and activities to gain an understanding of key principles and to assess both the relevance and application of critical realism as a tool for critical thinking in relation to health and social care.

Chapter aims

- To examine the concept of critical realism as a means of critical thinking in health and social care
- To promote reflection upon the relevance and value of critical realism to the context of health and social care

Learning outcomes

After studying this chapter, you should be able to:

- identify the key concepts associated with critical realism
- critically discuss contemporary issues in health and social care using critical realism
- evaluate the use of critical realism as a critical thinking tool in the context of health and social care

Critical realism: key concepts

Critical realism emerged through dissatisfaction with two key paradigms of how the world is viewed; namely, through a 'positivist' perspective or a 'post-positivist' approach. As McEvoy and Richards (2003) note, critical realism is an approach that combines a realist ontological perspective concerning the nature of 'being' alongside a relativist epistemology of how knowledge is constructed. In essence, critical realists eschew notions of radical relativism underpinned by a post-positivist tradition – in which all truths are held to be real and thus equally valid – whilst recognising that positivist perspectives of observable scientific certainty are also fallible and subject to being shaped by the conceptual frameworks in which scientists operate. The idea of fallibility of scientific reason is one also shared by post-positivists such as Popper (1992) who argues that 'effective' science seeks to disprove findings rather than replicate more of the same in order to generalise. Key figures in the European critical realist movement include Rom Harré, Roy Bhaskar and Margaret Archer. Hammersley (1995) suggests that its US counterpart 'scientific' realism has also become an influential movement that criticises both relativism and its opposite force, empiricism, in which only that which is observable is considered real.

In order to judge the validity of critical realism as a theory that transcends mere dissatisfaction and deconstruction, it is necessary to gain some understanding of the key facets of all three views regarding the nature of scientific evidence that is positivism, post-positivism and critical realism.

Key facets of a positivist/empiricist stance

- Scientific knowledge is proven knowledge
- Scientific theories are derived from the facts of experience acquired by observation and experiment
- Science is based upon what can be experienced by the human senses
- Science is objective
- Scientific knowledge is reliable knowledge because it is objectively proven

Key facets of a post-positivist/relativist stance

- Knowledge evolves constantly
- Theories are developed from experience, meaning and relationships
- Knowledge is based upon the meanings given to certain phenomena
- Meanings are subjective, unique and interpreted according to individual experience
- Knowledge is reliable, according to each individual, as part of their interpretation of 'sense-making'

Key facets of a critical realist stance

- The world keeps turning, thus developing understanding of the turning world is complex
- Some knowledge can be made 'real' via observations
- Knowledge development and production are complex processes
- All structures in the world have meaning
- Certain structures are catalysts for making things happen
- All occurrences are relative to context
- Scientific processes are not neutral
- Linguistic mechanisms are central to knowledge processing

Activity

Consider each of the above stances.

- Do you agree with any of these sentences?
- Which (if any) are problematic?
- Do they follow in a logical order?
- Can critical realism successfully fuse together elements of both positivist and post-positivist perspectives?

McEvoy and Richards (2003) outline Bhaskar's notion of the four key constituents that make critical realism a feasible yet robust alternative to both positivism and post-positivism. These comprise: searching for generative mechanisms; acknowledging the stratified character of natural and social worlds; examining the interplay between social structures and humans; critiquing of the existing social order.

Searching for generative mechanisms

This concerns exploring the below-the-surface processes that contribute to what is seen as real in appearance. Critical realists imply that although these generative mechanisms are not directly observable, they are still 'real' as their effects emerge at the surface. When adopting a critical realist position, there are some differences assigned to causation that deviate from those offered by positivists. Critical realism explains causation as being time and space dependent, thus the natural world operates as a multi-faceted open system in which generative processes may remain dormant until activated by particular contexts. This produces the equation of 'context + mechanism = outcome', compared with a positivist account which accepts broadly that 'action + mechanism = outcome'.

Real-world example: The status of volcanic activity, in which the overall physical presence of the volcano, and the potential activity beneath, may or may not cause an eruption: the eruption does not have to be observed or experienced in order to understand its potential as real; in health and social care, detection of the genetic markers for breast cancer and ovarian cancer can lead to treatment prior to any physical dysfunction. The cancer does not have to be diagnosed for the risk to be perceived as real.

The stratified nature of natural and social worlds

This element concerns the multi-layered character of both natural and social worlds in which these causal mechanisms operate. It recognises that any physical reality experienced can also be mediated by socio-cultural construction at societal, organisational and individual levels. The concept of ageing can be offered as one example to highlight this process: there is the physical and biological evidence of bodily change that can be documented and observed; there is the wider reality of how different cultures perceive the ageing concept with great variation – as something to deny, avoid or battle against – or as something to be valued, respected and welcomed; there are economic conditions which stratify the experience of ageing, such as whether there is full access to social welfare provision, adequate pensions and income. Thus many layers and processes can influence the empirical reality.

Real-world example: The constructed nature of disability, in which a person living with a disability may be disadvantaged economically by having limited work opportunities; this could be due to a range of causal mechanisms, including: restrictive government policy-making; employers' lack of insight into their capabilities; lack of physical resources and access to assistive technologies; the lived experience of their disability per se.

Interplay between social structures and humans

Tensions exist between material and behavioural explanations of lived experience. Materialists in a Marxist tradition, view structural inequalities as the key mediating variables of how life is experienced, regardless of the perceptions held by individuals about their own circumstances; hence, access to good housing, education, overall lifestyle and social welfare is influenced by the relationship to capital and power and the ways in which the social and material infrastructure privileges certain social groups. This compares with behavioural, or agential, approaches which place greater emphasis on the ways that humans respond to circumstances and to the attached meanings they construct in account; cognitive restructuring is a direct example of this approach. Critical realists straddle this dichotomy, believing that there is interdependency between both structure and agency that has to be acknowledged. Material structures provide resources that can enable and/or limit individual behaviours; yet human behaviour is not fixed immutably to such structures, as individual agents can have the capacity to transform the parameters of their material world in addition. The historical context also influences this facet, as Archer (1995) notes, the lived reality includes a legacy of structural conditions inherited from past contexts.

Real-world examples: Membership of the social 'underclass', in which a constellation of material, socio-cultural and perceptual influences determine both the label and relative chances for individual reassignment; in health and social care, the lived experience of diabetes as a long-term condition can be mediated by how individuals adapt and by the resources available to them. The disease process may be similar yet the outcomes can be very different.

Critiquing the existing social order

Critical realism does not adopt a one-dimensional socio-political agenda to explain fully the existing social position. In keeping with the overarching commitment to pragmatic pluralism, it offers analyses utilising several sources of socio-political explanation. Hence, it uses some Marxist theory to explore the socio-economic influences that have a tangible effect on real-life experiences, yet it also recognises some validity in post-structuralist notions regarding the use of political ideology to control belief systems of individual agents, as removed from structural impact.

Real-world examples: 'Third Way' political analysis attempts to critique real-world phenomena using a range of material and perceptual sources in explanation; in health and social care, the drive for inter-professional or multi-disciplinary ways of working, is underpinned by the need to use different approaches to ensure its effectiveness and evaluation.

Activity

Consider each one of the four key constituents of critical realism, as described above.

- Can you identify one 'real world' example for each aspect?
- Which, if any, of the four dimensions is the most useful?

According to Houston (2001) Bhaskar's work has an emancipatory momentum, in addition to his conceptual beliefs: 'For Bhaskar, a moral imperative exists in all social scientific work: if we discover human suffering of any kind through our research or practical endeavours, then we must consider ways of removing that suffering' (p. 224). This is taken forward through a process of 'retroduction' in which the investigator will seek to identify emerging patterns of behaviour that appear to illustrate underlying need.

This process builds upon the concepts of induction, in which perceptions are drawn from experience, and deduction, in which perceptions are developed from axioms, accepted laws, conventions and logic. A key principle of critical realism concerns acceptance that methods of inquiry can only ever achieve a partial understanding of the real world; this may be refined to obtain a 'truer' picture, yet it will never result in a complete grasp of reality. This perspective eschews notions of positivist truths alongside recognising that total relativism yields little explanatory value.

Patomäki and Wight (2000) contend that critical realism can ameliorate conceptual tensions between an epistemological standpoint of *how* things are known that is knowledge acquisition, and the ontological emphasis concerning *what* is known that is the nature of existence/being or reality. They suggest that adopting an anti-realist stance is not productive, yet deciding upon the type of realist to become may yield tangible results: this is the fertile ground that critical realism can cultivate effectively. Patomäki and Wight (2000) state:

> According to critical realism, the world is composed not only of events, states of affairs, experiences, impressions, and discourses, but also of underlying structures, powers and tendencies that exist, whether or not detected or known through experience and/or discourse. For critical realists, this underlying reality provides the conditions of possibility for actual events and perceived and/or experienced phenomena. (p. 223)

Patomäki and Wight (2000) do not accept that critical realism merely provides: mid-point compromise for the two oppositional forces of positivism and post-positivism. They argue that if the opposing forces are conceptually flawed, then exploring a 'middle ground' basis for two wrongs does not aid either cogent analysis, or further philosophical understanding: 'a synthesis based on two problematic metaphysical systems produces only a synthesis of two 'problematic metaphysical positions – not an improved metaphysical position' (p. 215). Interestingly, they contend that the diametrically opposed views of the positivist 'world out there' and the post-positivist 'world all in here' are not that dissimilar when applying an ontological focus: the common denominator shared by both is a commitment to an anti-realist stance.

Positivism only recognises that which can be observed and experienced as 'real', anything else is fictitious. However, the authors advocate that the aligning of existence to experience implies an agent capable of doing the experiencing; hence, the conclusion that there can be no experience without somebody 'real' to experience it. Equally, Wight (1999) notes that post-positivism maintains that nothing exists outside of discourse and linguistic construction; yet post-positivist theorists still reify the notion of 'nothing' by devoting much of their analyses to deconstructing its 'reality'!

Table 8.1   Key differences between positivism, post-positivism and critical realism

Key questions	Positivism & Empiricism	Post-positivism & Relativism	Critical realism
What is a human being and what is the nature of the social world?	Based in 'apparent' realism (observable & physical)	Based in relativity (mutable & process-based)	?
How are human beings related to their social world?	Deterministic (hierarchically ordered)	Voluntaristic (ordered via a series of relationships)	?
What counts as valid knowledge?	Objectively constructed (Value-free)	Subjectively constructed (value-laden)	?
How can we create knowledge?	Nomethetic process (or deductive)	Ideographic process (or inductive)	?

Activity

Consider Table 8.1, detailing some of the key differences between positivist/empiricist views and post-positivist/relativist notions.

- Using the above contentions to assist you, fill in the gaps using a critical realism perspective

---

Clearly the ground occupied by critical realists is also shared with some other perspectives and theorists. In the early 1980s, the physicist, Fritjof Capra (1983) published 'The Turning Point' in which he identified that the relationship between the natural world and human activity needed redefining. He suggested that the fixation with orthodox science, as being the only reliable source of establishing truth, needed to be abandoned and replaced by a new paradigm. His work emerged from a 'new physics' movement that rejected ideas of absolute or objective knowledge. The parallel with critical realism develops further in relation to Capra's view that the scientist cannot be separated from any experiment but is inextricably linked: subject and object are therefore part of the same process. Neither can cause and effect be treated simplistically, as Capra (1983) contends that change occurs due to a network of prevailing factors rather than through linear one-dimensional routes. This aligns with a critical realist view that cause and effect notions are part of a bigger system in which social relations and infrastructures influence what is made 'real' that is generative mechanisms relating causation as being both time and context dependent.

However, a further distinction should be made between the philosophical underpinnings of critical realism, with its commitment to the privileging of ontology, alongside the proliferation of 'mixed method' approaches which have emerged as part of a supposed paradigm shift. As Sapsford and Jupp (1996) note, mixed methods are used primarily to validate data rather than to explore philosophical standpoints. Hence, mixed methods approaches are often linked directly to a technical rationalist need for validity and rigour, not to exploring deeper ideological underpinnings that may be implied superficially. Wai-chung Yeung (1997) suggests that whilst critical realism provides an invaluable insight into wider philosophical and ontological debates, it has not yet addressed adequately how such philosophical clarity can be transformed into a distinctive practical methodology, owned as a critical realist approach per se.

Application of critical realism to contemporary issues in health and social care

Given the growing prominence of critical realist application to a range of social research areas, its use within a health and social care context continues to increase. The concept of wellbeing provides an interesting challenge for critical realism application. As Seedhouse (1997) notes, a cogent definition of wellbeing has been sought for decades that is acceptable yet embraces a range of dimensions including social, physical, spiritual and emotional facets. Attempts to define wellbeing have ranged from: the World Health Organisation's (1946) constitutional definition of complete health as: 'a state of complete physical, mental and social wellbeing and not merely the absence of disease or infirmity' which dwells upon recognising a broader focus for wellbeing than just a lack of dysfunctionality; to the approach of Shah and Marks (2004) who advocate a two-dimensional model of individual wellbeing, comprising: 'Life satisfaction – captures satisfaction, pleasure, enjoyment and contentment. Personal development – captures curiosity, enthusiasm, absorption, flow, exploration, commitment, creative challenge and also, potentially, meaningfulness' (p. 4).

The latter captures perfectly the growth of Beck and Beck-Gernsheim's (2003) notion of a contemporary society built around individualization, in which the individual must take active control of all the services and provisions needed for a unique and worthwhile life. However, as Beck and Beck-Gernsheim (2003) note:

Individualization is a social condition which is not arrived at by a free decision of individuals . . . people are condemned to individualization. Individualization is a compulsion,

Table 8.2 Critical realism applied to wellbeing

Critical realism descriptor	Wellbeing application
The world keeps turning	People have enduring social and physical wellbeing needs and expectations
Developing an understanding of the turning world is complex	Context and understanding play key roles in wellbeing outcomes and aspirations
Some knowledge can be made 'real' via observations	Wellbeing is reified via social processes
Knowledge development and production are complex processes	Building a concept of wellbeing is complex and evolving
All structures in the world have meaning	People have an opinion about wellbeing, regardless of its personal relevance
Certain structures are catalysts for making things happen	There are some fundamental elements that impact on both social and physical wellbeing
All occurrences are relative to context	People make and take lifestyle choices in accordance with meeting their perceived needs
Scientific processes are not neutral	Conventional wellbeing approaches are underpinned by specific agendas
Linguistic mechanisms are central to knowledge processing	People are sold lifestyle 'choices' through jargon, expert knowledge and persuasive social marketing techniques

> albeit a paradoxical one, to create, to stage manage, not only one's own autobiography but the bonds and networks surrounding it and to do this amid changing preferences and at successive stages of life, while constantly adapting to the conditions of the labour market, the education system, the welfare state, and so on. (p. 4)

They do not view this emphasis towards an individualised context as liberating for the many; rather, they imply that for most individuals, the responsibility for self-fulfilment that each has to manage within the global neoliberal economy replacing the state, will damage wellbeing not enhance it. These contested wellbeing indicators are then conjoined with some new emphases emerging from the changing economy, including: gene manipulation and supposed 'pre-dispositions'; behavioural and environmental adaptations; the development of a global and transient economy. Critical realism is well placed to provide an analytical framework for assessing some of the competing wellbeing claims and realities. Table 8.2 outlines a broad overview of how critical realism can be applied to wellbeing analyses.

The world keeps turning: This implies that there is a level of physical certainty that constructs an acceptable reality. When applied to wellbeing analysis, there is recognition that both individuals and populations alike have enduring social and physical needs and expectations. There is a set of assumptions made about the minimum pre-requisites demanded for a worthwhile existence, regardless of whether citing the WHO Ottawa Charter (1986) which speculated that people could begin to take more control over their own lives through three key processes of mediation, enablement and advocacy; or when using the Human Rights Act (1998) in which 16 basic rights, ranging from matters of life and death to those affecting everyday existence are recognised as basic entitlements.

Developing an understanding of the turning world is complex: Context and understanding of an acceptable reality are key mediators of wellbeing outcomes and aspirations. Both Marmot (2005) and Wilkinson (1996) observed that relative context and perceived hierarchical positioning had tangible influence upon peoples' sense of social standing, perceived health status and measurable physical indicators of health. Whereas the Black Report (1980) and the subsequent update by Acheson (1989) argue that specific material circumstances are highly influential for overall wellbeing outcomes. Marmot (2005) and Wilkinson (1996) contend that individual perceptions of abilities, social positioning and sense of self-determinacy contribute substantially to the lived experience of wellbeing, regardless of the material circumstances of everyday existence.

Some knowledge can be made 'real' via observations: Because pursuit of 'wellbeing' is viewed as being part of an inevitable quest for human self-improvement, any help offered in assisting the achievement of elevated health and social standing, is expected and anticipated. This public display of overt self-care, whether via further study, attending fitness classes, or through any combination of 'healthy' lifestyle choices, becomes part of the social fabric in which those seeking higher level wellbeing are valued as being socially responsible; their efforts are then reified through a range of social processes indicating wider approval. As Seedhouse (1997) notes, 'good life' health promotion becomes embedded in social processes that make self-care notions real, desirable and motivating.

Knowledge development and production are complex processes: Building a coherent and comprehensive concept of wellbeing is both complex and dynamic. Seedhouse (1997) suggests that pursuit of wellbeing per se is a red herring, given that so many versions exist which claim to have discovered its very essence: 'psychologists interested in finding out more about wellbeing are not searching for an independently existing thing, rather they are attempting to manufacture a helpful notion or concept. The notion of well-being does not exist separately from human beings' theories about it, and so cannot be discovered in the way that the relationship between heat, volume and pressure can' (p. 118). An interesting advance on this notion concerns the supposed identification of the 'real' constituents of happiness; manifested by a growing number of university departments researching into the application of 'positive psychology' skills, alongside Seldon's (2006) exploration of integrating the teaching of happiness within the UK mainstream secondary education curriculum.

All structures in the world have meaning: Regardless of its personal significance, individuals have an opinion about wellbeing concerning, relative access, its components, and social status conferred via its acquisition. Wilkinson and Marmot (2005) contend that just as social and material infrastructure impacts upon perceived wellbeing, the converse can also be applied, in which the lived experience of an individual's overall wellbeing and health status influences their opportunities for social mobility.

Certain structures are catalysts for making things happen: There are some key facets that influence social and physical wellbeing, ranging from Maslow's (1971) stepped approach to notions of self-actualization, in which basic pre-requisites involving essential physical need fulfilment are satisfied, followed by emotional needs fulfilment. He argued that only then can individuals progress to have sufficient self esteem to enable full 'self actualization', comprising: personal achievements, creative expression and self-fulfilment. This structured approach is then built upon by Antonovsky (1987) who contends that instead of looking at deficit models regarding lack of wellbeing, theorists should adopt a salutogenic perspective in which factors assisting people to remain well should be focused on, alongside seeing stressors and disruption as unavoidable and as part of a normal life pattern, rather than as malevolent structures and occurrences.

All occurrences are relative to context: Epidemiology is the study of population health and associated disease patterns; its evidence base exerts a powerful influence on the wellbeing agenda. According to Trichopoulos (1996) the main aim of epidemiology is to: 'decipher nature with respect to human health and disease' (p. 436). Epidemiology is also about assumptions, premised on predictions of population health trends and human behaviour; however, this perspective fails to account for ways that people make lifestyle choices which meet their own personal 'logic' rather than following the expected 'herd' behaviour for wellbeing enhancement. Jones and Sidell (1997) contend that human knowledge cannot follow a stringent, predictive quality, in which all contextual factors are excluded. They cite individual calculations of risk, the evolving nature of wellbeing expectations and the changing attitudes towards 'professional' expertise as key mediators of lifestyle choices. Such processes render the 'illogical' as entirely 'logical' when assessed on an individual basis. In alignment with a critical realism perspective, Jones and

Sidell (1997) recognise the relative nature of daily living, calling for: 'more sensitive methods for exploring and understanding the social context of people's lives' (p. 262).

Scientific processes are not neutral: Findings from the Black Report (1980) and a multiplicity of further studies clearly demonstrate a link between structural inequality and wellbeing deterioration; three decades later, acceptance of this reality is still contested. The economic impact of reducing widespread inequalities, whilst enhancing universal wellbeing, is far too costly for any elected government existing within a neoliberal economy that seeks to reduce state intervention into social affairs. Wellbeing research is not impervious to wider agendas, as illustrated by the privileging of evidence based practice as key predictors of wellbeing intervention 'effectiveness'.

Linguistic mechanisms are central to knowledge processing: The development of the world-wide web has had a marked effect on individuals' willingness to challenge existing knowledge bases alongside exploring whether 'expert' status is justified. The population is sold 'appropriate' lifestyle choices through a combination of jargon, expert knowledge and sophisticated social marketing techniques. The values of wellbeing are also assumed; in relation to both the physical output indicators that high level wellbeing demands and the assumption that everybody desires 'wellbeing' regardless of whether individual behaviours indicate contraindicated action.

Table 8.3 provides an illustration of how specific practice-based outcomes – in this example, public health – can be applied to a critical realism examination of wellbeing.

Activity

Tables 8.2 and 8.3 illustrate how critical realism can be applied to a specific aspect of health and social care. For example, 'wellbeing' and application to some practice-based outcomes for public health.

- Match each of the generic CR descriptors to a particular facet of health and social care that is significant to your professional domain
- Now identify some tangible practice-based outcomes that could result from your application of a critical realism perspective

Table 8.3 Critically 'realistic' public health?

Critical realism descriptor and wellbeing application	Public health outcomes
The world keeps turning People have enduring social and physical wellbeing needs and expectations	Some form of public health system will always be necessary
Developing an understanding of the turning world is complex Context and understanding play key roles in wellbeing outcomes and aspirations	Public health workers (PHW's) should understand the importance of context to people's lives
Some knowledge can be made 'real' via observations Wellbeing is reified via social processes	Key health beliefs endure and should be acknowledged
Knowledge development and production are complex processes Building a concept of wellbeing is complex and evolving	PHW's should recognise that many authentic versions of wellbeing may exist at the same time; they may also undergo considerable mutation
All structures in the world have meaning People have an opinion about wellbeing regardless of its personal relevance	Members of the population hold legitimate insight into wellbeing across a range of contexts
Certain structures are catalysts for making things happen. There are some fundamental elements that impact on both social and physical wellbeing	Wellbeing status is determined primarily by structural factors beyond individual control
All occurrences are relative to context. People make and take lifestyle choices in accordance with meeting their perceived needs	Lay epidemiology should be given equal worth alongside professional views
Scientific processes are not neutral. Conventional wellbeing approaches are underpinned by specific agendas	PHW's are conduits of social manipulation. Cause and effect evidence relating to wellbeing should be offered judiciously
Linguistic mechanisms are central to knowledge processing People are sold lifestyle 'choices' through jargon, expert knowledge and persuasive social marketing techniques	The language and ethical underpinning of public health persuasion needs to be demystified and made more transparent

Chapter summary

This chapter has considered some of the key concepts associated with critical realism, ranging from its emergence from dissatisfaction with existing world views that offered only partial explanation, to examining notions that it operates more effectively as a philosophy rather than as an active methodology. Patomäki and Wight's (2000) contention that critical realism is more than the sum of positivism and post-positivism (described by the authors as two 'wrong' perspectives) illustrates the potential for critical realism to remain impervious to the more basic discussion concerning mixed method approaches to inquiry; in remaining an essentially philosophical perspective, it does at least avoid getting bogged down in disputes about salience of pragmatic application.

Roy Bhaskar's contribution to a critical realism perspective is acknowledged, especially through his work in determining the four key analytical constituents, comprising the search for generative mechanisms, stratified nature of both natural and social worlds, the interplay between social structures and humans and the critiquing of an existing social order. When applying 'real-world' examples to his constituents, the perspective becomes a useful tool for reconciling some of the key assumptions that stymie sense-making of the social and natural elements of the world, as experienced.

A critical realism critique of wellbeing and the allied activity of public health practice, illustrates how a physically experienced phenomenon can be conjoined to socially constructed processes and infrastructures without irreconcilable outcomes. Given the tensions implicit in health and social care concerning the accommodation of corporeal, social and economic 'realities' within a coherent professional domain, the instrumental use of this theory to help unpack and acknowledge the critical uncertainties should not be underestimated.

Sources of further reading and exploration

Books and journals

Archer, M., Bhaskar, R., Lawson, T. and Norrie, A. (eds) (1998) *Critical Realism: Essential Readings*. London: Routledge.

Bhaskar, R. (1979) *The Possibility of Naturalism: A Philosophical Critique of the Contemporary Human Sciences*. Brighton: Harvester.

Capra, F. (1983) *The Turning Point*. London: Flamingo Books.

McEvoy, P. and Richards, D. (2003) 'Critical realism: a way forward for evaluation research in nursing?' *Journal of Advanced Nursing*, 43 (4): 411–420.

Sayer, A. (2000) *Realism and Social Science*. London, Thousand Oaks and New Delhi: Sage Publications.

Web

Cambridge Realist Workshop: hosted by Department of Economics, Cambridge University. It emphasises methodological and philosophical debates about the nature of science. Available at: www.econ.cam.ac.uk/seminars/realist/

Centre for Critical Realism: supports practical and theoretical activities concerned with the development of realist social theory and philosophy. Available at: www.criticalrealism.demon.co.uk/

International Association for Critical Realism: international networking resource for all interested in realist philosophy. Coordinates the annual international conference and produces the *Journal of Critical Realism*. Available at: www.criticalrealism.demon.co.uk/iacr/

9

CHAOS AND COMPLEXITY THEORIES

Liz Smith and Stella Jones-Devitt

This chapter explores chaos and complexity theories and discusses their use as critical thinking tools in health and social care. It provides an overview of the key concepts of chaos and complexity theories and offers critical analysis of these theories as critical thinking tools. Activities and exercises are designed to assist with the application of theory to practice and identify the relevance of chaos and complexity to health and social care at a clinical, management and organisational level.

Chapter aims

- To provide an overview of the key concepts associated with chaos and complexity theories
- To promote reflection upon the relevance and value of chaos and complexity theories to health and social care

Learning outcomes

After studying this chapter, you should be able to:

- identify the key concepts associated with chaos and complexity theories
- critically analyse links between chaos and complexity theories
- critically discuss contemporary issues in health and social care using chaos and complexity theories
- evaluate the use of chaos and complexity theories as critical thinking tools in health and social care

Chaos theory: key concepts

Chaos theory was first discovered by Edward Lorenz, a meteorologist, in 1961. It has however been contemplated for a several millennia in the history of mankind. It can be identified as a concept in early religious philosophy such as Hinduism (Lorenzen, 2002) and the nature of chaos in the universe was considered by Isaac Newton. Chaos itself has differing meanings and is often perceived as meaning 'disorder' or 'confusion' as identified in many dictionaries (e.g. Oxford, 1998). However, in the context of chaos theory this is not what is meant. Chaos theory relates to systems which are sensitive to initial conditions. This is sometimes referred to as the 'Butterfly Effect' as described, for example by Stewart (1997):

The flapping of a single butterfly's wing today produces a tiny change in the state of the atmosphere. Over a period of time, what the atmosphere actually does diverges from what it would have done. So, in a month's time, a tornado that would have devastated the Indonesian coast doesn't happen. Or maybe one that wasn't going to happen, does. (p. 141)

This in effect means that chaotic systems will react to a small change in a way which can lead to growing errors in predicting future behaviour (Gollub and Solomon, 1996). Lorenz discovered this when he attempted to run his weather prediction programme to view a particular sequence again. Instead of starting at the beginning of the sequence he started from the middle and to save paper set it to print out to three decimal places not the usual six. This small difference should not have had any effect on the sequence by the conventions of the time however the result was very different from the original.

Chaos theory is therefore related to the principles of non-linear dynamics which can be illustrated by some simple mathematics (Warren, Franklin and Streeter, 1998). Take a series of numbers, for example, 1, 2, 3, 4 and multiply each by two and repeat this with the result. The result is a predictable and linear one as 1, 2, 3, 4 becomes 2, 4, 6, 8 which then becomes 4, 8, 12, 16. This would produce a straight line if plotted on a graph as the difference between the numbers gets larger but is proportionately the same each time. If however, the same numbers are multiplied by themselves rather than two the picture is very different as 1 squared always remains 1; however 2 squared becomes 4, which becomes 16 which in turn becomes 256; 3 squared becomes 9, which becomes 81 which in turn becomes 6561. A small change in the initial number has a large impact on the end result and the progression is non-linear.

Chaos theory does not only have relevance to mathematics, physics, meteorology and sciences generally, but can also be related to the more social sciences. This is perhaps clearly illustrated in some popular films about human relationships, for example, 'Sliding Doors' (1998) or the classic 'It's a Wonderful Life' (1946). Both these films develop the theme that small events can have far-reaching and unpredictable effects. 'Sliding Doors' shows the two parallel lives of the heroine and how they differed depending on whether she managed to get on the train before the doors closed or not. 'It's a Wonderful Life' has James Stewart being shown by the angel that he has in fact had a positive and previously unrecognised impact on many lives in his community by means of showing him how things would be if he had never existed. The community was significantly changed and was not the pleasant place he knew. These fictional and somewhat 'feel good' movies provide examples of the non-linear relationship between small actions and their consequences. This can be applied to both individuals and to organisations where a single decision about an aspect of the organisation can have a much wider effect than anticipated.

Chaos theory therefore relates to effects which are seemingly random, however, they are not truly so. Rambihar (2004) makes a link with cricket where there are non-linear interactions between the weather, ground conditions and selection policies and other factors in determining outcomes but a single shot may ultimately decide which team win. The shot cannot be predicted in relation to its occurrence or indeed in its effect on the outcome. However, that effect is not random in the sense that if one team are five runs behind in the dying moments of the match and the batsman hits a six then his team will win, nonetheless if he is bowled out the result is completely different.

Activity

- Do small events in your everyday work make a big difference over time?
- Consider this in relation to events which may have affected you as an individual, your immediate team or colleagues and the organisation.

Complexity theory: key concepts

Complexity theory builds on the principles of chaos theory. The study of non-linear dynamics has given rise to the recognition that many living systems demonstrate chaos and that this leads to complex behaviour (Warren, Franklin and Streeter, 1998). This complex behaviour can be seen in individual organisms, ecosystems and human interactions. Complexity theory suggests that within organisations there is a zone of chaos and anarchy and a zone where behaviour is linear and rational and between these two zones lies the zone of complexity. Within the zone of complexity there is a complex adaptive system consisting of a number of individuals who behave according to their own principles (Burgess, 2004).

Plsek and Greenhalgh (2001) set out some basic concepts of complex adaptive systems. They suggest that the individual agents within the system are free 'to act in ways which are not always totally predictable, and whose actions are interconnected so that one agent's action changes the context for other agents' (Plsek and Greenhalgh, 2001, p. 625). Complex systems have 'fuzzy boundaries' with a membership which can change and agents can be members of several systems simultaneously. This can be seen in any human organisation however small as its members will also be involved in other 'systems' such as their family, social groupings, voluntary organisations, religious groups, etc. Within complex systems agents use internalised rules which govern action but may not necessarily be shared, explicit, logical or even fixed. An example which could be seen to illustrate this could be the internalised rules within a family – each will behave in a certain way in a certain situation but the internalised rule which governs that behaviour may not be shared. A shared meal can therefore be a mutual behaviour but the rationale for attending may be different for each member of the family and may change for the next meal.

Systems can be embedded within other systems and can co-evolve hence within an organisation a need within one system may result in the evolution of another to meet that need and both systems will alter to address the interdependence of each. For example, the purchase of a new piece of equipment within an intensive care unit will cause a change within the maintenance team who provide technical support, a change in the mode of working of a social care team will have an impact on the associated administrative support and each will co-evolve. This influence of one system within the organisation on other system(s) leads to tension and paradox and, in contrast to reductionist thinking, complexity theory accepts and even values this tension. The relationships within complex adaptive systems are non-linear and behaviour is emergent and sensitive to small changes therefore the system as a whole is subject to inherent unpredictability. However despite the unpredictability some overall patterns will be evident as some things will happen regularly although it will not be possible to predict the exact nature of the event, for example everyone in the family mentioned earlier will generally need to eat however they may not always eat together or the same number of times.

A concept which is often associated with complexity theory is that of attractors (Livneh and Parker, 2005). Plsek and Greenhalgh (2001, p. 627) describe attractor patterns as providing 'comparatively simple understanding of what at first seems to be extremely complex behaviour'. The beating of the heart and its associated beat-to-beat variation is offered by several authors as an example of an attractor pattern (e.g. Parker, Schaller and Hansmann, 2003; Livneh and Parker, 2005). Plsek and Greenhalgh (2001, p. 627) also offer the example of the psychotherapy client who will accept counselling advice more readily if it is framed in ways which enhance their 'core sense of autonomy, integrity and ideals'. Attractor patterns can therefore be used to understand what makes agents within the system 'tick' even though their behaviour may appear very complex.

Despite their unpredictability complex systems can demonstrate order and innovation from within. This occurs as there are simple, shared internalised rules within the system that create an element of self organisation without external direction. This allows the system to demonstrate creativity without falling into disorder and confusion.

Activity

- What 'systems' do you belong to?
- How do you think they interact and affect one another?
- Can your behaviour in one system be explained by the impact on you of another?
- Consider one system you are a member of – what internalised, local rules are there? Are there inherent patterns of behaviour within the system?
- Can you identify any changes that have occurred in one of your systems as a result of development or change in another system you are not a member of?

Links between chaos and complexity theories

Complexity theory is generally seen as an expansion on chaos theory in order to apply it to the social sciences. Complex systems are described as having the sensitivity to initial conditions that is identified in chaos theory. This, in turn, not only leads to non-linear dynamics within the system which causes inherent unpredictability, but also to creativity and innovation. However, since complexity theory relates mainly to systems and organisations there are additional ideas about the individual agents within the system, which although they are still linked to chaos theory are also more than simply a development of it. Just as there are films which illustrate chaos theory there are also some which are representational of both theories. One such was the much acclaimed 'Crash' (2004) which examines the events and interactions which led to the crash and its associated consequences amidst a background of racial tension.

Because of the close links between the two theories they are often discussed together in their application to critical thinking, for example in Livneh and Parker's (2005) discussion of the psychological adaptation to disability.

Contemporary issues in health and social care using chaos and complexity theories

Health and social care across the world has become more complex as technological advances are made, the practitioners involved develop more diverse and specialised skills and the organisations catering for need become larger and more bureaucratic. In addition to this, expectations of health and social care in the developed world have also grown exponentially whilst the needs of the undeveloped nations continue to increase. This growing complexity can lead to confusion, frustration and disillusionment both among practitioners and the users of the services. However it is possible that greater understanding of chaos and complexity theories could offer reassurance that all is not truly disordered and impossible to manage. These theories can offer different ways of thinking, which could prove helpful in unravelling the problems faced by those involved in health and social care on an individual, organisational and possibly global level.

It can be argued that practice, organisation, information management, research education and professional development are interdependent and that the systems which involve these issues are interacting with each other (Plsek and Greenhalgh, 2001). It is therefore feasible that the conceptual frameworks needed to make sense of these systems should be dynamic and emergent rather than reductionist. The concept of organisations being 'machine-like' and therefore big problems can be solved by reducing them into smaller component parts is perhaps no longer sufficient for practitioners at all levels of health and social care to ensure delivery of a high-quality service to patients and clients. The following section will therefore consider how understanding and decision-making may be enhanced by the use of chaos and complexity theories.

Wilson and Holt (2001) suggest that human beings are not only agents within complex systems but are in themselves complex and adaptive systems. Each individual has multiple interacting physiological systems which are self-regulating. This means that any system failure has an impact on the other systems of the body and therefore cannot be treated in isolation. This is sometimes recognised in the more acutely ill patients/clients but not always in the chronically ill. Models of care have been criticised for being reductionist in nature and addressing the disease rather than the patients as a whole. However seeing the patient/client as a physiological whole is not sufficient in itself for making sense of their needs and understanding behavioural responses. Each human being is an agent in a range of systems which will influence their behaviour. They will have relationships with other individuals and within society which will have an effect on their values and beliefs which in turn will influence their behaviour in response to their health and social care needs. Relationships may change and evolve and this may have an unpredictable effect on the individual. Care therefore needs to be holistic in nature and accept that unpredictability will be a feature of the interaction between the patient/client and the services provided. There needs to be a flexible and emergent approach to care which recognises that not only the biological, psychological and social needs of the patient/client will change but also that a change in one element will have an impact on the others which may be apparently disproportionate.

Activity

Joe is a diabetic. He is 56 years old and has only recently been diagnosed. He is a widower and has two married sons who live in the local area. He works as a self employed gardener and enjoys an evening in the pub after work where he often meets up with his sons. His GP and the specialist nurse have tried to make Joe understand the importance of dietary control and a reduction in his alcohol intake however he appears not to want to comply with their plan of care.

- What might be influencing Joe's apparent failure to comply with his health care advice?
- What are the systems involved?

Andrea is 19 years old and a student living in University accommodation. She suffers from anorexia nervosa and is seriously underweight. She has an older brother who is a successful lawyer and a much younger sister who is the 'baby' of the family. Her parents are supportive however they have difficulty understanding Andrea's problems. She is an intelligent young woman who has the potential to gain a good degree. Her poor diet has led to gastro-intestinal problems and she is experiencing hair loss as a result of nutritional deficits. Despite support from her GP and a mental health team Andrea's overall health is deteriorating and she continues to perceive that she is fat.

- What are the interacting systems in Andrea's care?
- How is each impacting on the other?

Health and social care practitioners are themselves part of a number of complex systems. Their personal systems will have an impact on their work lives as well as those systems directly related to their practice. It is easy to say that workers should leave their personal lives at home but less easy to do. It is also true that each individual will behave according to the beliefs and values they have as a result of their relationships and culture outside their work place. Nonetheless the systems they work within need to be understood better to be able to maximise the service offered to patients and clients. One of the significant issues in modern health and social care is the diversity of roles within services and the difficulties experienced when these roles interact.

The notion of inter-professional working is high on the political agenda currently however it is also a very practical issue whether it is seen as a policy priority or not. The need for good working relationships and communication can be seen in any number of important health and social care issues such as child protection, care of the older person, care of adults and children with learning disabilities, teenage pregnancy, drug misuse, etc. It is clear however that within the complex systems of health and social care working relationships and interactions between groups of practitioners is essential to quality service delivery. Understanding the complexities of the systems within services and the unpredictability of their behaviours is necessary to improve inter-professional working and break down the barriers to effective communication.

Activity

Doris is 75 years old and has diabetes. She lives in a residential nursing home provided by Social Services. She has a vascular leg ulcer which requires regular dressings by the Community Nurse. She also requires regular foot care which is not currently available from an NHS source therefore it has to be paid for each time. She is on medication for both her diabetes and to control her high blood pressure. Doris has recently developed signs of dementia and is being assessed by the Community Mental Health nurses at the request of her GP.

Consider the number of different practitioners involved in the care of Doris.

- What problems might arise in achieving seamless care for Doris?
- How might complexity theory assist in solving these problems?

The case study of Doris demonstrates the complexity of delivering a seamless service to patients and the problems associated with the different and interacting systems involved. Each of the systems will have its own internalised rules and patterns of behaviour which will not necessarily easily adapt to each other. However consideration of attractors may be of use in this type of situation so that co-ordination of care can be organised by framing it in ways which are congruent with all systems.

In addition to the consideration of the delivery of quality services health and social care practitioners are increasingly required to address risk management. Risk management is defined by the NHS Executive (1999) as a means of reducing the risks of adverse events occurring in organisations by systematically assessing, reviewing and then seeking ways to prevent their occurrence. Assessing risk can be improved by acknowledging the interaction of the systems involved. Risk is rarely straightforward, situations which allow occurrences such as Beverley Allitt or the Bristol cardiac surgery deaths are not just about the single nurse or the surgical team but are complex and involve many systems which have an impact on the whole situation.

Consider, for example, the risk analysis of a lone practitioner working in the community in areas where crime and violence are not uncommon. The risks are not simply related to being a single person in a violent area but are also related to whether the practitioner is known, how they appear (obvious uniform or incongruent dress), whether they appear to be carrying drugs or other items worth stealing (attractor patterns) and the time of day. A number of systems interact to create a potential risk and the solution must also address these systems, pairing practitioners for instance in some situations may increase rather than decrease the risk as a pair may be perceived as a greater threat.

Management and leadership of health and social care have clear resonance with the concept of chaos and complexity. Management, like medicine, has often been reductionist in nature as the notion of the organisation as a machine made up of separate, independently functioning parts being a central precept. Targets and changes are often introduced into individual elements of service without there being any consideration of the whole picture. Consider, for instance, the four-hour target for Accident and Emergency Units (A&E). This target was set to reduce the time patients spent in A&E before being sent to a ward or discharged and came about in response to scenes of patients waiting hours for a bed on trolleys in corridors. However the target does not take into account the complexity of the original problem which had as much to do with a lack of beds on the wards as it had to do with lack of organisation in A&E. The target makes no attempt to address the complexity of the problem but rather puts pressure on staff that has little control over the causes of it. Additionally the target does not consider the individual needs of the patients, for some patients four hours is far too long, for others it is little more than an inconvenience to wait longer.

The picture is further complicated by events in primary care as patients increasingly find that they cannot see their GP out of hours and therefore more attend the local A&E for non-urgent symptoms. Complexity theory complements the notion of strategic thinking where the 'bigger picture' is contemplated to allow for effective planning. Tackling a single element of the system by setting a target or changing the way of working cannot hope to solve a problem as complex as waiting times however applying complexity theory and considering the interactions which give rise to the problems may offer a better opportunity to improve not only the situation in A&E but also other problems which have an effect on patient movement within a hospital.

Activity

- Consider a problem in your area of work. What are the contributing factors to that problem and how many systems are involved?
- Do you belong to all the other systems involved?
- Can you control the behaviour that contributes to the problem?

Plsek and Wilson (2001) also suggest that considering attractor patterns may be a better way of managing change than dealing with resistance. They argue that change needs to be communicated in a way which is meaningful to those you wish to change and offer the example of a GP who does not follow guidelines, who will not be influenced by their evidence base, but will probably respond to information relating to the relevance of the guidelines to his patient population.

Activity

- Consider a change you have experienced. What, if anything, encouraged you to accept the change?
- What about others who were affected by the change – did they have a different view of what was positive about it?

Utilising an approach to management and leadership, which acknowledges that the organisation cannot be separated into constituent parts but needs to be considered as a set of interacting systems is also in line with the concepts of inter-professional working which are now very much a feature of health and social care. Just as considering patient/client care in this manner can encourage a more inter-professional approach so can management and leaders encourage a more cooperative approach to organisational problems by perceiving the interactions between the differing professions and social groupings within the institution. It can also encourage service-user involvement by understanding that users are an adaptive system which interacts and affects the overall organisation.

Chaos and complexity theories have been identified as having relevance to education in general and therefore to education within health and social care. Lorenzen (2002) summarises the relevance of chaos theory to education and describes the teacher and the students as agents of chaos. He argues that each teaching session is uncertain despite careful planning, that there will be an infinite number of occurrences that can affect the outcomes of the session. This can be seen in the context of practice-based teaching where it is not always possible to plan teaching and learning opportunities or to avoid disruptions. The links between teaching and learning can often be difficult to perceive as students learn in a non-linear way and at different paces from each other. Approaches to teaching can appeal to some students and not others; equally there are external factors which will affect both teacher and students at any given time. Education within health and social care needs to be flexible and able to adapt to the complexities of the interaction between the systems involved (students, teachers, patients/clients, the learning environment, the organisation, etc).

There also needs to be an understanding of the interactions of classroom-based learning and practice-based learning to avoid the classic theory–practice gap. Learning about the legal and policy elements of child protection, for example, are insufficient to prepare a practitioner to deal with the reality. Practice experience cannot always provide the learner with the necessary scope of knowledge and skills therefore innovative approaches are needed to encourage problem-solving and sharing of experiences in small groups. Fraser and Greenhalgh (2001) argue that it is the very complexity of health and social care which makes it a requirement to ensure that education within it addresses the need for practitioners to have capability as well as competence. Practitioners they argue need to be able to adapt to change and to apply their knowledge to new situations (Fraser and Greenhalgh, 2001). Lorenzen (2002) suggests that teachers need to accept chaos and prepare for it. He also argues that whilst chaos brings uncertainty it also provides opportunity for creativity and hope.

Chaos and complexity theories as critical thinking tools in health and social care

The previous section has discussed some potential applications of chaos and complexity in relation to health and social care. The principles of the theories in relation to decision-making are that the 'cause and effect' relationship is rarely straightforward. Health and social care of necessity involves human beings and their interactions. Decision-making, whether at a practice base or management level, therefore needs to take into account the complex, dynamic and often unpredictable nature of the interactions of the physiological and psychological systems in a single individual, the social interactions of individuals be they patients/clients or staff and the systems within the organisation.

Complexity theory can offer the practitioner an alternative view to the reductionist approach to patient/client care and help to understand what often appears to be irrational behaviour by encouraging a more holistic approach which accepts unpredictability (Wilson and Holt, 2001). A criticism of this approach could be that chaos and complexity theory relates to deterministic systems, yet human beings have free will (Warren, Franklin and Streeter, 1998). However free will is inevitably subject to the constraints of biology, culture and society and results therefore in non-linear behaviour.

Chaos and complexity theories have relevance to the management of change both at practice and management levels. The change agent needs to understand the systems which interact with and affect the system he/she wishes to change and to consider the applicability of the evidence base of the change to the current situation given the systems involved. Many change-management theories rely on Lewin's seminal work in which he asserts that there are three stages to change: Unfreezing, Moving and Re-freezing (Burnes, 2004). Lewin also recommended the use of force-field analysis to map driving and restraining forces. Understanding the systems involved can be very useful when considering drivers and restraints to change. Plsek and Wilson (2001) also identify how complexity theory can be useful in motivating people into accepting change by considering attractor patterns rather than taking a 'command and control' approach to resistance to change.

Complexity theory can be applied to strategic thinking in health and social care. Mintzberg (2000) considers that 'seeing' is the most important factor in developing strategy; seeing ahead, behind, from above and below, beside, beyond and seeing it through. This relates to the idea of the 'bigger picture' which requires one to take into account the wider ramifications of a strategy which can be supported by means of understanding the systems involved and their interactions with each other. In a target-driven service as is being currently experienced in health and social care it is vital that strategy takes into account the complexity of the implementation of policy as otherwise the target will not be met which defeats the original objective.

Chaos and complexity theories have much to offer practitioners of health and social care both at a 'grassroots' level in assisting with the understanding and planning of patients/client care and at organisational level in relation to change management and strategy development. The organisations involved in health and social care delivery are large and complex, practitioners and managers' alike need to understand how this impacts on their decision-making and rather than being perceived as a threat to the development of innovative approaches to quality care it can be seen as an opportunity to a more holistic way of thinking.

Chapter summary

Chaos and complexity theories offer an alternative to the reductionist mode of thinking which sees individuals and organisations as 'machines' made up of separate, constituent parts which can be considered in isolation from each other. It is in keeping with the ethos of critical thinking which encourages intellectual enquiry and innovation. It is also congruent with a shift towards holistic approaches to care and towards developing effective strategies to support the delivery of care and the implementation of policies designed to improve the quality of care. It acknowledges the uniqueness of the individual and each situation and helps practitioners understand that a small change can have a large and often unpredictable impact highlighting the need for flexibility and adaptability at an individual and organisational level.

Sources of further reading and exploration

Books and journals

Fraser, S. W. and Greenhalgh, T. (2001) 'Coping with complexity: educating for capability', *British Medical Journal*, 323: 799–803.

Lorenzen, M. (2002) *Chaos Theory and Education*, www.libraryreference.org/chaos.html

Plsek, P. and Greenhalgh, P. (2001) 'The challenge of complexity in health care', *British Medical Journal*, 323: 625–628.

Plsek, P. and Wilson, T. (2001) 'Complexity, leadership and management in health care organisations', *British Medical Journal*, 323: 746–749.

Stewart, I. (1997) *Does God Play Dice? The Mathematics of Chaos*. Harmondsworth: Penguin.

Warren, K., Franklin, C. and Streeter, C. L. (1998) 'New directions in systems theory: chaos and complexity', *Social Work*, 43 (4): 357–372.

Wilson, T. and Holt, T. (2001) 'Complexity and clinical care', *British Medical Journal*, 323: 685–688.

Web

www.horsesenseatwork.com/psl/pages/chaosdefined.html
http://en.wikipedia.org/wiki/Chaos_theory
www.soc.surrey.ac.uk/sru/SRU18.html
http://complexity.orcon.net.nz/

10

POSTMODERNISM AND POST-STRUCTURALISM

Peter Draper and Stella Jones-Devitt

This chapter considers some of the major concepts and debates associated with postmodernism and post-structuralism. It provides an overview of key ideas underpinning postmodernism and post-structuralism and their development as theories, alongside exploring some of the key differences between postmodernism and its counter perspective, modernism. The chapter covers the overarching themes that prevail, assisting the reader through specific activities to gain an understanding of key principles and to assess both the relevance and application of postmodern and post-structural accounts as tools for critical thinking in relation to health and social care.

Chapter aims

- To explore key concepts associated with postmodernism and post-structuralism
- To promote reflection upon the relevance and value of postmodernist and post-structuralist perspectives in the context of health and social care

Learning outcomes

After studying this chapter, you should be able to:

- identify the key concepts underpinning postmodernism and post-structuralism
- critically analyse similarities and differences between modernist and postmodernist perspectives
- critically discuss contemporary issues in health and social care using postmodernist and post-structuralist perspectives
- evaluate the use of postmodernism and post-structuralism as critical thinking tools within the context of health and social care

Postmodernism: key concepts

From time to time a term arises which expresses a range of meanings about an historical period and the ideas and cultural practices current within it. For instance, the term 'Renaissance' is used to describe the development of art and literature in Europe in the fourteenth to the sixteenth centuries; the term 'Enlightenment' to describe the thinking of eighteenth-century philosophers such as Descartes and Bacon. Typically, terms such as Renaissance and Enlightenment do not simply refer to the products of individual disciplines such as painting, literature or philosophy, but to inter-related sets of ideas which cross disciplinary boundaries. For instance, the ideas developed by Descartes, Bacon and other philosophers had an impact on the development of scientific method. This led to a period of enormous cultural confidence: technical and theoretical problems were solved and there seemed no limit to the capacity of the Western mind to understand nature and impose order on society, as old forms of knowing based on religion or tradition were superseded by science. Thus terms such as Enlightenment do not simply describe abstract ideas but tend to spill over into other aspects of life; it seems reasonable to describe them as having cultural, as well as purely philosophical, meanings.

Postmodernism is such a term. According to Appignanesi and Garratt (1999) it was first used in the late nineteenth century, since when it has been applied to painting, literature, architecture, photography, philosophy, sociology and many other fields of study. The first objective of this chapter is to explore its meaning.

Establishing the foundations of postmodernism, concerns assessing the impact of modernism, scientific thinking and language. A number of writers define postmodernism in relation to a prior approach known as 'modernism'. Mannion and Small (1999) suggest that the modernist approach is to assume that the problems faced by human beings can be solved primarily by the application of rational, scientific thinking: the modernist regards science as an approach that will lead to an expansion in overall knowledge, bringing with it an ability to understand and thereby control the world.

Klages (1997) develops this idea further, arguing that modernism is based on the following views:

- that each human being is a stable, coherent, knowable self that is rational and autonomous
- the use of rational reasoning enables the self to know itself and the world in an objective way
- science can produce universal truths about the world
- the facts identified by science are true in all places and at all times

- science is neutral and objective, and science stands as the paradigm for any and all socially useful forms of knowledge
- language is also rational, with a firm and objective connection between the objects of perception and the words used to name them

Creek (1997) continues in this theme as she provides a useful account of the basis of modernist thinking:

Since the 17th century, Western science has been progressing steadily towards discovering the laws that govern the universe. As the scientific method achieves greater accuracy, reliability, objectivity and rationality, so we approach closer to the goal of absolute knowledge. This is the enlightenment vision, which began with Descartes, although its roots can be traced back to Plato . . . This has become a metaphor for Western philosophy, which engages in linear arguments to prove that there are values that exist independently of a particular culture or society. Human beings have the capacity to achieve an abstract, universal standpoint from which they can attain true knowledge and understanding of the workings of the universe, including the workings of the human body and the human mind. (p. 50)

Activity

- To what extent does modernism describe the basic assumptions of scientific medicine as it is practiced in the National Health Service?
- Consider Klages' list, above, and see if it 'matches up' to your area of practice

---

Arguably, 'modernism' captures quite accurately the current emphasis in the British NHS on evidence-based medicine. This can be illustrated by considering several of Klages' key points:

- Science can produce universal truths about the world
- The facts identified by science are true in all places and at all times

In Chapter 4, Sackett et al.'s (1996) influential definition of evidence-based practice was considered, in which 'evidence' was defined as: 'the conscientious, explicit, and judicious use of current best evidence in making decisions about the care of individual patients' (p. 71). Their further definition of 'best evidence' is noted as referring to:

clinically relevant research, often from the basic sciences of medicine, but especially from patient centred clinical research into the accuracy and precision of diagnostic tests (including the clinical examination), the power of prognostic markers, and the efficacy and safety of therapeutic, rehabilitative, and preventive regimens. External clinical evidence both invalidates previously accepted diagnostic tests and treatments and replaces them with new ones that are more powerful, more accurate, more efficacious, and safer. (p. 71)

This definition clearly rests on a scientific world view corresponding closely with 'modernist' assumptions. Consider another of Klages' key points:

- Science is neutral and objective, and science stands as the paradigm for any and all socially useful forms of knowledge.

Activity

- To what extent does modernism describe the basic assumptions of evidence based practice?
- Consider Klages' list, above, and see if it 'matches up' to your area of practice

---

There is little acknowledgement in the wider literature of scientific medicine of possible limitations to the scientific method. Often, the universal validity of scientific approaches is simply taken for granted in an unquestioning way. In this way, complex conceptual and psychosocial phenomena such as stress, depression, quality of life and spirituality are subject to measurement techniques, serving as outcomes in randomised controlled trials, whilst little thought appears to be given to the validity of this approach.

- Language is also rational, in that there is a firm and objective connection between the objects of perception and the words used to name them

This is a very important point; its significance emerges more clearly when considering the concepts of post-structuralism and deconstruction, below. Both of these concepts, and the assumption addressed in the bullet point above, address the relationship between the reality experience as part of the 'lived' world, and the language used to express that reality. Such concepts challenge the easy assumption that the role of language is simply to provide labels whose purpose is to enable descriptions of what occurs in the world. This important point merits further explanation.

Burrell and Morgan (1979) suggest there are two fundamental ways of understanding how language is used to describe the world: through 'realism' and 'nominalism'. The immediate concern of this chapter is not to express a preference between these two approaches, but to enable an understanding of their relative meanings.

Realism considers that 'objects of thought' (a term which refers to just about anything) exist independently of any attempt to investigate or know about them. This is a 'common sense' view. For instance, it is obvious that a chair being sat upon does not depend for its very existence upon somebody thinking about it, or needing to ascribe a word for it.

The contrasting view is known as 'nominalism'. This notion contends that there is no independently accessible 'thing' which constitutes the meaning of a word and thus a definitive object. The nominalist is not denying that a chair exists, but suggests that the only reason 'chair' can be used as an example is due to having an accepted vocabulary of words and language for chairs: without the word 'chair' there would be no way of discussing this phenomenon. For the nominalist, language does not just provide a way of describing what is going on in the world; language is so central to an overall experience of the world that without it, there would be no world to describe.

Activity

Consider the concept of nominalism:

- What does it mean to suggest that language is so central to our experience of the world that without it, we would not have a world to describe?

Postmodernism invites thinking about the 'world' in a limited sense and has sought to provide an analytical framework for everyday lived experiences and even for 'trivia'. It avoids large-scale macro analyses of the globe spinning through space, seeking instead to dwell upon a more limited and familiar 'world'. For example, it might consider the 'world' of football, or line-dancing, or budgerigar breeding. Each of these 'worlds' has its own set of interests (who will win the world cup), terminology (the off-side rule) and social practices (such as going to football matches) which are deeply familiar to those who inhabit that world, but completely hidden from those who don't.

This more limited concept of 'world' can be applied across a range of professional 'lives'. Taking the 'world' of nursing as an example, incumbents are socialised into the nursing profession and become familiar with 'nursing' ways of looking at things. In the early 1980s, a series of developments occurred which brought into being a new 'world' of nursing which would have been entirely unfamiliar to practitioners of an earlier generation, as the concept of 'the nursing process' was introduced to the profession.

The nursing process was a new approach to organising care which involved the systematic assessment, description, intervention and evaluation of patients and their problems. The nursing process soon developed its own terminology, research base, and ways of practicing, and everybody in the profession had an opinion about it. In the mid-1970s, there was no such thing as the nursing process, but 10 years later a 'world' had come into existence which had its own vocabulary, practices and world view. This illustrates the postmodernist position concerning ways in which language can be used to create a new 'world'.

Similarities and differences between modernism and postmodernism

Thus far, postmodernism has been defined against the background of a former approach known as modernism. 'Scientific' thinking has been characterised as modernist, whilst different ways in which language might be used to describe and construct the world has also been explored; yet, telling little of the 'positive' content of postmodernism in terms of its key assertions and primary authors. Rolfe (2001) gives a useful account of the key concepts, linking them with significant writers on postmodernism and providing a starting point for further exploration.

The first concept Rolfe discusses is postmodernism itself. Rolfe suggests that the relationship of postmodernism to modernism is not principally a temporal one: postmodernism is not simply that which follows modernism, as might be implied by the prefix 'post'; rather, the relationship between modernism and postmodernism is a critical one which actually assumes that modernism and postmodernism will exist, although uncomfortably, side by side. Rolfe also suggests that one of the clearest definitions of postmodernism is found in the work of Lyotard (1984) who said: 'simplifying to the extreme, I define "post-modern" as incredulity towards metanarratives' (p. xxiv).

As this definition suggests, the concept of the metanarrative is a key one in postmodernism, and its meaning will now be addressed. It should also be noted that the terms 'metanarrative' and 'grand narrative' are used interchangeably in the literature. Alvesson and Skoldberg (2000) provide a definition of the term metanarrative and explain its linkages to postmodernism:

> Since the 1970's, especially under the influence of Lyotard's book, The Postmodern Condition (written in 1979), the term 'postmodernism' has become more and more common. Here, the front line is drawn . . . against a metaphysical inheritance of ideas, which is asserted to pervade all Western tradition from Plato onwards, and which especially has found expression in the eighteenth-century Enlightenment movement – the

birth of modernity: the notion that there are some rational, global solutions and explanations, some general principles which guarantee progress in the development of knowledge. According to postmodernism, though, these are not what they are asserted to be, but rather kinds of myths or 'grand narratives', rhetorically coloured, dominant discourses that should be replaced by micro histories – always provisory and limited stories. Claiming to be no more than they are, these micro histories at the same time do not try to repress the power aspects, frictions, contradictions and cracks which unavoidably emerge in any discourse, either openly as in postmodernism or covertly as in metaphysics. (p. 148)

Postmodernism entails rejecting the view that human beings have access to 'objective' standpoints that enable judgments to be made about the truth or falsity of propositions, statements or claims: instead, each society is seen to be sustained by a series of metanarratives. Narrative is the act of story-telling and story-telling involves the creation of complex and compelling, but ultimately illusory, worlds. Metanarratives can thus be defined as stories a culture tells about itself. It is important to note that metanarratives have a legitimising function (Rolfe, 2001) with one of their key functions being to explain why things are as they are. Klages (1997) offers some illustrative examples: the grand narrative in American culture might be that democracy is the highest and most rational form of government and that eventually it will lead to universal human happiness; the corresponding grand narrative for Marxism would be that capitalism will eventually collapse to be replaced by a socialist utopia.

Postmodernism, by reclassifying monolithic intellectual and social systems as metanarratives, challenges their claims to universal validity and truth. This has implications for our understanding of science, and also for social institutions and practices which justify themselves in terms of science. Science, to the postmodernist, is not to be regarded as the only valid approach to truth. Science may have its own internal logic and procedures of evidence, but fundamentally it is limited in its range, local in its relevance, and recent in its history.

So far, some of the differences between modernist and postmodern approaches have been considered. Table 10.1 puts some of these issues side by side for comparison.

It was suggested above that metanarratives have a legitimising function, implying that their purpose is to justify or explain why things are as they are. It follows that for the postmodernist, metanarratives are linked to the possession and the exercise of power. Rolfe (2001) contends that the relationship between knowledge and power emerges in the concept of authority. The word 'authority' is used in two senses. Sometimes, authority is associated with being knowledgeable, in the sense that one might 'be' an authority. Alternatively, authority can imply being powerful, in the sense of 'having' authority.

Table 10.1 A comparison of modern and postmodern thinking

	Modernist	Postmodern
Reasoning	Generated from a basic foundation of facts and scientific truths	Multiple factors impact upon multiple layers of reasoning and shifting realities and truths
Science	Founded on universal optimism and a belief that the scientific method can lead to truth	A limited view of science which doubts the possibility of universal truth and contextualizes scientific knowledge
Part/Whole	Parts comprise the whole 'Grand/Meta Narrative'	Whole is more than the parts – if it exists. 'Micro Narrative'
Language	Realist. Language is used to stabilise and provide a normative framework	Nominalist. Language is socially constructed and meaning reflects the social context of its use

Post-structuralism: key concepts

The terms postmodernism and post-structuralism are sometimes used synonymously, but it is probably more accurate to regard post-structuralism as a sub-set of postmodernism (Mitchell, 1996; Seidman, 1994). The difference is one of focus, for as Cheek (2000) notes: 'postmodern analyses tend to be wider in scope (and) focus on aspects of culture, society and history, post-structural studies have tended to concentrate on analyses of literary and cultural texts, where text refers to a representation of any aspect of reality' (p. 40).

It should be noted that 'text' does not just refer to words printed on a page, although of course it includes texts of this kind. Pieces of art, web pages, buildings, transcripts of interviews and music can all be regarded as textual. This is why Rolfe (2001) draws on the work of Derrida (1974) to argue that writing refers: 'not only to the inscription of symbols on a page, but also to cinematography, painting, music, sculpture, sport, politics, cybernetics, and life itself. Thus, a text (what is written) also takes on extended form as a shorthand for all attempts at representation' (p. 43).

The term 'text', then, is a flexible one, going far beyond the written page. It may be helpful to consider if and how the term can inform thinking about the professional practice of health and social care. For many practitioners in health and social care, the human body can usefully be thought of as a text. Holland and Adkins (1996) contend that the body has now gone far beyond mere representations of functionality, becoming instead a vehicle for exploration of human subjectivity. They state that it has become: 'a mixture of both matter and discourse' (p. 121).

Activity

In everyday life, a 'text' is thought of as some words on a page, whether it be a bus ticket, a shopping list or a text book. The primary way in which texts are used concerns reading them for information; this is done by scanning the marks on the page and simultaneously interpreting them to arrive at the meaning. A similar process of 'reading' can be used to scan and interpret the human body during the processes of professional care.

- Identify the features of the human body that would be significant to you in your professional work (e.g. the presence of a bruise)
- Assess these in relation to the various interpretations you might make of each of these features (low platelet count, a recent fall, a sign of deliberate harm, an injury during sport)
- Reflect on how you would arrive at the 'correct' interpretation in each case
- Does the notion of the human body as text add anything to your understanding of this process of interpretation and professional judgement?

The exercise above suggests that the process of 'reading' a text can be ambiguous, as the meaning of a particular text might be subject to several competing interpretations. This is obviously the case in the interpretation of a physical sign such as a bruise, but it also applies to the understanding of written texts, which can be equally ambiguous.

This notion aligns closely with the concept of 'discourse', because the discourse in which we are located will influence approaches to the text. The starting point is to recall a point that was made above in the discussion of 'worlds'. Revisit the suggestion that the world of football has its own set of interests (who will win the world cup), terminology (the off-side rule) and social practices (such as going to football matches) which are deeply familiar to those who inhabit that world, but completely hidden from those who don't. These interlocking phenomena help to illustrate the concept of discourse, which is used to express integrated ways of thinking, talking, and acting, and the values underpinning them.

The term discourse can be applied in various ways. Rolfe (2001) relates it to the academic world, suggests that 'discourse' refers to the assumptions made and the (usually) unwritten rules used to arrive at the 'correct' interpretation of the subject matter of an academic discipline or field of study (Rolfe, 2001).

Grbich (1999) gives a more clinical example, contending that discourses are 'dynamic dialogues' in which meaning is socially produced, reproduced and transformed in interaction:

> The discursive practices of a hospital ward, for example, include case notes, treatment modalities, and interaction among health professionals and between health professionals and patients. These practices are linked to others, both structural and ideological, within the hospital, which are in turn linked to practices in the wider society. All of these discursive practices make up the order of discourse within a particular domain, within which practices and particular discourses can be identified. (p. 153)

Arney and Bergen (1984) give another, complementary definition of discourse, also drawn from medicine. They suggest that discourse:

> is more than just a set of facts known by physicians and embodied in a professional, specialized, inaccessible language. The medical discourse is a set of rules that enables facts to become facts for both physicians and patients. It is a set of rules that covers not only what is important to doctors but also what patients can speak about as important. Knowledge is power precisely because the knowledge embedded in the medical discourse supplies rules by which patients ascertain when they are speaking true about the self and when they are speaking about things that are imaginary. Knowledge tells the person what is important and not fanciful about his or her experience of illness and patient hood. (p. 5)

In summary, as Mitchell (1996) suggests, post-structuralism highlights the role of language in organizing the subjective self and social institutions, and it demonstrates how language is used to empower and privilege certain individuals, groups and forms of social life.

This chapter has presented an account of postmodernism and post-structuralism in which the concept of 'discourse' has been given a prominent place. The concept of discourse demonstrates the relationship between language, power, authority and social practice. In this context, 'deconstruction' has been developed as an approach to highlighting these relationships as they are manifest in texts.

According to Rolfe (2001) deconstruction: 'aims to uncover the hidden meanings in a text, often by teasing out contradictions in seemingly innocuous marginalia, since it is in the digressions and asides rather than in the well rehearsed key passages of the text that an author often gives away conflicting beliefs' (p. 43).

There are many examples of the use of deconstructive techniques in health and social care literature. See for instance Hall (1999) and Stevenson (2001).

Contemporary issues in health and social care using postmodernism and post-structuralism

The preceding account of postmodernism and post-structuralism shows how language, knowledge, authority and power can form a nexus which influences both experience and understanding of health. An example is drawn from Jordan (1977), a social anthropologist who has explored in some detail, the ways in which authoritative knowledge is produced and validated in the field of human reproduction (obstetrics and midwifery). Her work explores the creation and validation of authoritative knowledge, whilst explaining how it is linked to the exercise of power; although she does not refer specifically to postmodernism, Jordan's approach displays many of the features of a postmodern analysis.

Jordan's principal argument is that several different systems of knowledge are likely to exist for each field of human interest. She suggests that typically, some systems of knowledge are regarded as being more credible than others, either because they seem to offer a better or more useful explanation of the domain in question, or because their advocates have a stronger power base, or perhaps both. Sometimes, parallel systems of knowledge exist, and people are happy to move between them, perhaps using them in parallel or sequentially. Jordan introduces the term 'authoritative knowledge' to describe the outcome of a process that occurs when one form of knowledge takes precedence over others. She notes that, as a consequence of this process, other forms of knowledge may be devalued or dismissed and those who favour them may find themselves depicted as ignorant troublemakers who have nothing important to say. Jordan suggests that the creation of authoritative knowledge is a social process which creates and maintains the balance of power within the relevant community. Typically, most of the members of that community will believe that the way things are is a reflection of some natural order that ought not to be challenged:

Authoritative knowledge is persuasive because it seems natural, reasonable and consensually constructed. For the same reason it also carries the possibility of powerful sanctions, ranging from exclusions from the social group to physical coerciveness . . . . Generally, however, people not only accept authoritative knowledge (which is thereby validated and reinforced) but also are actively and unselfconsciously engaged in its routine production and reproduction. It is important to realise that to identify a body of knowledge as authoritative speaks, for us as analysts, in no way to the *correctness* of that knowledge. Rather, the label "authoritative" is intended to draw attention to its status within a particular social group and to the work it does in maintaining the group's definition of morality and rationality. *The power of authoritative knowledge is not that it is correct but that it counts.* (Jordan, 1997, pp. 57–58)

The area of pregnancy and childbirth is one in which competition between forms of knowledge can sometimes be observed. Historically, pregnancy and childbirth were considered to be natural and normal events. With increasing medicalisation in the nineteenth and twentieth centuries, childbirth came to be considered normal only in retrospect that is the identification of a birth as normal was only possible after the woman had successfully negotiated the events of labour and birth. Thus, the status of knowledge previously accorded to women was systematically removed and replaced by medical knowledge which gained its legitimacy at the expense of women's knowledge of their own bodies. The growth of 'natural childbirth' pressure groups emerged as a backlash to the privileging of such medicalisation; yet, whether this was based upon relativist notions of lay epidemiology, or merely represented a new micro-narrative version of 'universal truth' is open to further conjecture.

Activity

Consider the following observation about the NHS:

> Everywhere I go, the senior people tell me of progress, of better working methods and value for money, of objectives achieved, of changes delivered. Everywhere I go, I also glimpse another world, a world inhabited by everyone else – a world of daily crisis, and concern, of staff under pressure and services struggling to deliver. Both worlds are real in the minds of those who inhabit them. Both worlds are supported by objective evidence. Both views are held sincerely. (p. 192) (Ken Jarrold, cited in Hadley and Clough, 1996)

Explore the following questions, first in relation to the observation itself and then more broadly in relation to your own practice.

- What is really going on here?
- How can postmodernist/post-structural perspectives be helpful with critical analysis?
- What are the key criticisms of such theories?
- Think of an example from your own practice, in which applying PM/PS can be helpful?

A further example of the way in which bodies of knowledge are valued differentially in the health setting can be seen in the notion of 'lay knowledge'. The concept of lay knowledge refers to the knowledge that patients/clients have about their bodies as a result of their lived experience. The ascendancy of medical knowledge over all other forms of knowing often restricts the value that is placed on patients' or clients' own knowledge about their state of health or illness.

Postmodernism and post-structuralism as critical thinking tools in health and social care

Advocates of postmodern and post-structural approaches find that they offer powerfully subversive critical tools which expose sources of authority and decision-making as fundamentally self-interested. Critics, on the other hand, view them as an irrelevant, even harmful distraction from the important goal of scientific knowledge as the proper basis of professional practice. As postmodern and post-structural theoretical critiques are grounded in relativism and discourse, their application to practice can be equally ambiguous, as illustrated within the following activity.

Activity

Discuss the following views and determine which one you think is right:

1 Positive PM/PS application produces more fluid healthcare systems resulting in greater choice and flexibility; leading to greater ownership and involvement in service provision (e.g. the user as the 'expert', with recognition that professionals are users as well).

2 Negative PM/PS application sees the healthcare system as too fragmented, resulting in isolation of autonomous functioning and (paradoxically) greater internal rigidity; there are no discernible key principles in such fragmented organisations, thus providing a surveillance service rather than directly delivered provision; this produces an accountability paradox: too much administrative red tape and target indicators, whilst professional accountability becomes harder to measure and less responsible.

Regardless of such ambiguity, postmodern and post-structural ideas have brought new ways of sense-making in health and social care analyses, via their challenge to existing order and their deconstruction of privilege in social institutions and relationships. Paradoxically, given the determination to pursue a metanarrative explanation, postmodernism and post-structuralism appear to reflect much of the 'grand narrative' of contemporary neoliberalism. Heywood (2003) provides an account of the key facets of postmodernism, comprising analysis of: 'The shift away from societies structured by industrialization and class solidarity to increasingly fragmented and pluralistic "information" societies, in which individuals are transformed from producers to consumers, and individualism replaces class, religious and ethnic loyalties' (p. 323). Interestingly, this appears synonymous with the apparent apoliticism underpinning both neoliberalism and the pro-globalisation movement that is both premised on grand narrative principles.

Chapter summary

In this chapter, postmodernism and post-structuralism have been presented as counter reactions to the assumed certainty of scientific or objective efforts to explain reality; stemming from a recognition that reality is not simply mirrored in human understanding of it, but rather is socially constructed as the mind tries to understand its own particular and personal reality. Postmodernism and post-structuralism are highly sceptical of explanations which claim to be valid for all groups, cultures, traditions, or races, instead focusing on the relative truths of each person or group. In postmodern and post-structural understanding, interpretation is everything; reality only comes into being through unique interpretations of the world. Postmodernism relies on concrete experience over abstract principles, knowing always that the outcome of personal experience will necessarily be fallible and relative, rather than certain and universal. This chapter has also explored some key aspects of post-structuralist thought (derived from the deconstructionist philosophy of Derrida) which rejects the view that any text (material or corporeal) can have a claim to universal validity, on the grounds that their internal structural logic can be deconstructed.

Their use as evaluative tools of health and social care is contentious, with the underpinning relativistic ambiguity being seen as both a strength and a weakness; clearly, the influence in recognising the value of the micro-narrative of patient and service users' experience has led to a shift in perceptions of lay knowledge and the status of patient as 'expert'; in giving attention to the individual experience of social wellbeing and social malaise, these theoretical concepts afford connections with holistic, individualised approaches to care that modernism and universal truths cannot countenance. However, postmodernism and post-structuralism appear to have contributed minimally in application to wider structural analyses; it is acknowledged that this may be due to lack of insight about the scope of their use (alongside their pejorative positioning within the prevailing quasi-scientific domain) rather than because of any major conceptual flaws as critical tools.

Sources of further reading and exploration

Books and journals

Alvesson, M. (2002) *Postmodernism and Social Research*. Buckingham: Open University Press.

Appignanesi, R. and Garratt, C. (1999) *Introducing Postmodernism*. Duxford: Icon Books.

Derrida, J. (2001) *Writing and Difference*. London: Routledge.

Foucault, M. (1989) *The Birth of the Clinic: An Archaeology of Medical Perception.* London: Routledge.

Rolfe, G. (2001) 'Postmodernism for healthcare workers in 13 easy steps', *Nurse Education Today*, 21: 38–47.

Sackett, D. L., Rosenberg, W. M. C., Muir Gray, J. A., Brian Haynes, R. and Scott Richardson, W. (1996) 'Evidence based medicine: what it is and what it isn't', *British Medical Journal*, 312: 71–72.

Web

http://en.wikipedia.org/wiki/Postmodernism

www.colorado.edu/English/courses/ENGL2012Klages/pomo.html

www.michel-foucault.com/pomo.html

Section 3

**APPLICATION TO HEALTH AND SOCIAL
CARE PRACTICE**

11

CASE STUDIES IN HEALTH AND SOCIAL CARE

Liz Smith and Julie Dickinson

This chapter highlights some case studies in critical thinking and provides the reader with some differing methods of applying critical thinking skills to practice. Each case study has a distinct topic area; however, the topic has been selected to have relevance to broader aspects of health and social care. There should therefore be some resonance within the case studies for a range of practitioners in health and social care.

Chapter aim

- To promote the application to practice of selected critical thinking tools

Learning outcomes

After studying this chapter you should be able to:

- analyse contemporary issues in health and social care using multiple critical thinking tools
- evaluate the use of critical thinking tools in the context of health and social care

Case study 1: medical model or holistic care?

Rationale

The following case study utilises care of the woman during pregnancy and childbirth as a means to explore the debate about whether care planning should be organised around a medical model of care or be more holistic and individualised as per bio-psychosocial approaches to care. Maternity care is utilised as this has been a wide debate for many years within this sphere of health care and has involved not only health care professionals but also pressure groups, politicians and the public. It therefore has raised some clearly defined issues which lend themselves to critical analysis. These issues are not, however, unique to care of the woman in pregnancy and childbirth, but are relevant to many other areas of health and social care.

Maternity care has been subject to many changes over the twentieth century. Midwives, traditionally the main carers in pregnancy and childbirth, became 'registered' in 1903. This move which was intended by midwives to strengthen their position, actually brought them under the control of doctors who were responsible for their 'supervision' on the basis of safety. After 1905, the title of midwife could only be used by those already registered by the Central Midwives Board and those passing the Board's examination following a three-month training course. The National Insurance Bill of 1911, after successful lobbying by the Midwives Institute, included provision for childbearing women of free choice to decide whether to be attended by a midwife or a medical practitioner (Colwell and Wainwright, 1981). Parliamentary interest in improving maternal and child health continued, and in 1916 the training of midwives increased to four months for nurses and six months for those without nursing qualifications. This was in order to include antenatal care which was seen as a key factor in improving maternal and infant mortality (Robinson, 1990).

Throughout the 1920s and 1930s investigations by the Ministry of Health concluded that antenatal care was vital, and that antenatal clinics should be linked with maternity homes, to enable admission of those women requiring observation (Oakley, 1984; Robinson, 1990). During this period training for midwives was again increased to six months for nurses and one year for non-nurses. This was because statistics showed that 50 to 60 per cent of confinements were attended by midwives alone and therefore it was felt that training should be improved to account for this (Colwell and Wainwright, 1981). In the 1940s the Royal College of Obstetricians and Gynaecologists (R.C.O.G.) began arguing for maternity services to be focused on large hospitals under the leadership of a consultant. This debate continued throughout the 1950s during which time General Practitioners had taken over antenatal care and became the first point of contact for the pregnant woman with maternity services rather than the midwife, although by 75 per cent of women were still being delivered by a midwife (Robinson, 1990). In 1959, the Cranbrook Committee supported the R.C.O.G.'s view that 70 per cent of confinements should take place in hospital, and in 1970, the Peel Committee recommended that all deliveries should take place in hospital.

This move towards hospital confinement fragmented midwifery care between hospital midwives and community midwives, and in hospital, new maternity units were being designed with separate labour and delivery, and postnatal wards, further fragmenting care between midwives who gave care in labour and those who gave postnatal care (Robinson, 1990). In the Expert Maternity Group's (E.M.G.) report 'Changing Childbirth' (Department of Health, 1993) key aspects of care delivery were identified; namely, that care should be woman-centred, appropriate and accessible and that the service should be effective and efficient. This report advocated more choice for women in relation to where they delivered and also that there should be a move towards team midwifery to allow the woman to have a known midwife throughout pregnancy, childbirth and the postnatal period. Little has however changed and although there are some midwifery-led units, there has been scant increase in home deliveries whilst care in hospitals remains medically led and fragmented.

'Changing Childbirth' identified that 72 per cent of women would prefer an alternative to doctor-led hospital care and 44 per cent of these would prefer home delivery, however, the national figures for the UK home births indicate that between 1 and 8 per cent are achieved (Thornton, 2001). This is despite pressure groups such as the National Childbirth Trust (NCT), Association for the Improvement of Maternity Services (AIMS) and Association of Radical Midwives (ARM) campaigning for more woman-centred and socially supportive maternity services. Despite evidence to the contrary, politicians appear swayed by the medical view that childbirth is only 'safe' in hindsight and that hospital is therefore the best place for it to take place.

Thinking critically about medical model approaches and holistic care perspectives

Several critical thinking approaches will be used in this section to analyse the case study above. The intention is to provide a guide to the application of theory to an issue rather than to offer a detailed analysis of the medicalisation of maternity care.

Moral reasoning

Medicalisation of maternity care lends itself to analysis from a moral perspective as there are two main strands to the problem, namely the medical intention to prevent harm and enhance safety by hospitalisation, and the autonomy of women to decide what is best for them. The main approaches to this would therefore be to consider maternity care using the four moral principles advocated by Beauchamp and Childress (2001). The medical view on maternity services is that care should be delivered in an environment where risk is managed and therefore harm limited. This is perhaps paternalistic, but is arguably about addressing the fact that childbirth is not without risk to both mother and baby and that mortality and morbidity remain features of pregnancy and childbirth which politicians and pressure groups both wish to reduce to an absolute minimum.

It could also be considered from a utilitarian perspective as a moral action, since it is aimed at the 'greatest good for the greatest number' because of the emphasis on safety for the majority and also because society does generally view mortality and morbidity as being unacceptable; as shown by the vast sums paid in compensation with relation to Obstetrics. However the difficulty with the utilitarian approach is that it could be argued that the majority of women are not satisfied with a medical model of care, therefore utility is not being demonstrated.

The strongest moral argument against a medical model of care arises from the perspective of autonomy. Women are perceived to be denied choice and therefore do not have autonomy. Gillon (2003) places autonomy as 'first' among the four moral principles, as autonomous persons should decide on beneficence and non-malificence for themselves. Despite any good intentions by doctors and policy makers, it remains central to ethical care that women should make the informed choices. The majority of women going through pregnancy and childbirth are healthy women, completely able to make a rational decision about their own well being and that of their baby. Justice requires that all women have equal opportunity to exercise their autonomy in this respect.

Chaos and complexity

Chaos theory fits well with this issue, as one single change contributed to a number of potentially unanticipated effects. The move to hospital delivery, rather than home birth, had the effect of placing power and control into the hands of the doctors and in doing so ensured the medicalisation of childbirth. This may not have been problematic for women, but with it came a number of changes such as active management of labour, more pain relief and more surgical intervention. Hospitalisation made pregnancy and childbirth into an 'illness' instead of a normal physiological event.

The need to make childbirth safer, shifted from a need to have women in hospital to deal rapidly with any problems, to an active prevention of potential problems strategy. Childbirth is, however, a complex process and its outcomes cannot be predicted. Complexity theory can be used by either side of the argument in some respects; doctors would argue that the complexity of pregnancy and childbirth justifies their interventionist approach, while some women and midwives would argue that its very complexity makes it necessary to give the woman control over the process.

Feminism

This case study is ideal for analysis using feminist theory, as it involves debate between the 'masculine' scientific approach of medicine and the more 'caring' art of midwifery and motherhood. It could also be argued that it also relates to the classic notion of 'male' power and control over women who cannot be trusted to make rational decisions. Much has been written about the subject by feminist authors such as Ann Oakley and there is a wealth of material to draw upon in this respect. There is also scope for some links with moral reasoning in relation to the feminist ethic of caring, as described by Carol Gilligan. This type of case study could be used an illustration of how post-feminist theory may be flawed in relation to the fact that women have now 'got it all' as this clearly identifies that women still have to fight for the most basic right to have some control over their own bodies.

Application to other areas of health care

This case study can be related to many areas of health care as it highlights issues which are common to specialities other than maternity care. The power and control of medicine is by no means unique to obstetrics, and the issues relating to a 'masculine' scientific approach to care versus the more 'feminine' art of nursing, midwifery and some therapies, can be seen in many areas of health and social care. The debate regarding intuitive decision-making by 'expert' nurses illustrates these issues well. The case study also highlights the tensions in health and social care between choice, effectiveness and safety; as in a litigation-conscious society, these tensions will increase. Choice requires the acceptance of risk and the possibility of error, yet society in the Western world is not very accepting of human error in relation to health and social care, leading to 'defensive' practice that is less flexible and less individualised.

Case study 2: inter-professional working

Rationale

The following case study attempts to critically analyse the concept of inter-professional working within the framework of the 'National Healthy School Standard' (NHSS). The main source of information is the Standard's web site www.wiredforhealth.gov.uk which is referenced throughout. The case study will focus on 'Section 1' of the NHSS 'Partnerships' with its stated aim of: The local health schools programme must work in partnership at a strategic and operational level (Department for Education and Skills (DfES) and Department of Health (DOH) 2004: 3).

The National Healthy School Standard NHSS (www.wiredforhealth.gov.uk) is jointly funded by the Department for Education and Skills (DfES) and the DOH. It is part of the UK Government's drive to reduce health inequalities,

promote social inclusion and raise educational standards. Its philosophy is
that a healthy school is one that:

- is successful in helping pupils to do their best and build on their achievements
- is committed to ongoing improvement and development
- promotes physical and emotional health by providing accessible and relevant information and equipping pupils with the skills and attitudes to make informed decisions about their health
- understands the importance of investing in health to assist in the process of raising levels of pupil achievement and improving standards
- also recognises the need to provide both a physical and social environment that is conducive to learning

The NHSS is based on evidence that healthier children perform better
academically and that education plays an important role in promoting health,
particularly among those who are socially and economically disadvantaged.
(DfES 2001, DOH 1999). The NHSS guidance provides standards for local
education and health partnerships to guide the development of local healthy
schools programmes. The standards encompass partnerships, management
and working with schools. Information is also provided on a 'whole-school'
approach and specific themes (Department for Education and Employment
(DfEE) 1999, DfES 2005).

'Section 1.' of the NHSS 'Partnerships' is broken down into several key
standards, which include: the importance of an 'established' education and
health partnership; this mentions particular partners such as all school staff,
young people themselves and the involvement of statutory, non-statutory
agencies and community groups in the planning, delivery and evaluation of
activities. These standards also have more detailed 'components'.

Inter-professional working and the NHSS

This case study uses examples of particular projects from the scheme
(www.wiredforhealth.gov.uk sub-section 'case studies') to pull out specific
issues to do with inter-professional learning and working. The projects on
the scheme range from targeting the young people themselves with 'Teenage
health awareness days', a 'Multi-cultural week' and an 'Early years health
promoting project' to examples of working in partnership such as 'Working
with Connexions', 'Development of strategic links' and a 'Multi-agency
conference'. Other projects mentioned include 'Bidding for resources',
'Development of a PSHE and drug education policy', 'A Teenage pregnancy
strategy', 'Attracting funding' and 'Professional development of school staff'.
All these projects state very clearly that their main focus relates to the
standard of 'Partnerships' (DfES and DOH, 2004).

There is a high priority given to the importance of inter-professional
working, with clear strategic support from key players within the collaborating

agencies and professions; the work is an integral part of the organisations' business plans and not an 'add on'. Morrison et al. (2002) evaluated the pilot schemes and suggested that at an operational level, partnership working occurs, but that this is limited at a strategic level. Chalmers et al.'s (2004) evaluation of the related Personal and Social Health Education (PSHE) certificate programme noted that more recognition needs to be made at strategic level regarding the contribution of inter-professional working with schools.

Thinking critically about inter-professional working

Several critical thinking approaches will be used in this section to analyse the case study above. As before, the intention is to provide a guide to the application of theory to an issue, rather than to offer a detailed analysis.

Political and ideological perspectives

Historically, the importance of collaboration and cooperation between professions has been recognised since the early days of the Welfare State. However, as Taylor (1997) discusses, the move in the 1980s towards a market approach and increased competition for social and health services, hindered the process. This added to the formation of various barriers, both structural and cultural, including: control and accountability, differing ideologies, occupational cultures and the ignorance of other's roles. New Labour's approach however, seems to be once again supporting the early ideals of the Welfare State. The NHS Plan (Secretary of State for Health, 2000) required health authorities to develop Health Improvement Programmes (HImPs) which had to be in partnership with local authorities and others. These HImPs are highlighted in importance in the NHSS initial guidance (DfEE, 1999). Later policy diktats have replaced the HImPs with Local Delivery Plans (LDP) which implicitly abolish the requirement for partnership working with local authority; indeed, other partners are not even required to sign up in support of the plan (Evans, 2004).

Chaos and complexity

It can be clearly seen from examples within the literature, evaluations from projects, and research into this area, that this strategic approach is essential; so why does it continue to be a problem? The practicalities of working in partnership are central to the process. The issues include the importance of all stakeholders being involved from the start, using careful planning that clearly defines roles and responsibilities for all stakeholders. Chaos and complexity theories can offer some insight into why this type of partnership working may be problematic. The professional groups involved in the projects can be seen as complex adaptive systems which interact with one another, however they each function according to their own internalised rules which are not shared or necessarily understood between groups; hence, a small change in the way one professional group functions can have far-reaching and unexpected effects on the project(s).

Beattie (1995) explores these issues. He cites the following barriers to inter-professional working, including:

- disparities in organisational arrangements
- practitioners vary in how much autonomy they have in decision-making
- structures of accountability
- practitioners paid in different ways
- different budgets
- policy diktats from different sources

Postmodernism

All projects discussed under the heading 'Political and ideological perspectives' above cited the importance of being able to define clear outcomes associated with health, and the use of an evidence base which cites good practice. The NHSS is concerned with 'promoting health' but as discussed by Beattie (1995) the term faces a characteristically 'postmodernist' challenge, as there seems to be no single predominant set of explanations acceptable to all, no one master narrative that has universal assent, nor acceptance that multiple realities can be managed and accommodated in practical terms. The notion of agencies working together presents huge problems if the 'product', in this case, health, is not defined clearly, allowing for the sharing of common goals in working towards this. Government strategies may be seen to help with this (Department of Health, 2004), however, their translation in practice is still dependant on conflicting ideologies. This can be seen clearly in relation to the NHSS standards promoting the use of clearly defined health outcomes, alongside an education ideology of children and young people being empowered – indeed motivated – to make positive 'own' choices about their physical, emotional and educational wellbeing (Morrison et al., 2002).

Application to other areas of health and social care

This case study centres on the all important issue of inter-professional working. Increasingly, in health and social care, the professional boundaries are blurring, with a strong drive towards a much more patient/client-centred approach to care delivery, arguably ensuring that the person best able to provide care does so, irrespective of professional role. There is now a much closer link between health care and social care and this can give rise to problems relating to differing funding streams and diverse professional agendas. In addition, health promotion with the aim of preventing disease, rather than treating it, is very much an issue in the developed world; some of the issues highlighted in this case study will have resonance with a wide range of health and social care practitioners who have a remit to promote social wellbeing, whenever possible.

Case study 3: developing services for older people

Rationale

There has been a marked focus on health and social care services for the older person in recent times, largely due to the ageing population in the developed world, but also due to an increasing recognition that care of the older person has been something of a 'Cinderella service' which is long overdue for development. This case study therefore considers the issues associated with developing services which can be applied to either a practice or managerial perspective. The case study will, of necessity, take a 'broad brush' approach to the topic but will nonetheless present ideas which could be explored in more specific detail, according to the role of the reader. The policies discussed are from the UK, but relate to issues which are common to care of older people globally.

Care of the older person

Care of the older person has been the focus of health and social care policy in the UK; the National Service Framework for Older People (Department of Health (DOH), 2001) and the report of the Wanless Social Care Review team (King's Fund, 2006) are central features of this focus. There has also been media attention due to reports of abuse, concern that services are not responsive to the needs of older people, and financial disparity in relation to service provision between the four countries within the UK.

Older people can be construed as being vulnerable as they do not have a strong, representative voice, however there is an increasing trend in health and social care generally towards patient and service user involvement in service development; as a group, older people are raising their profile both by pressure groups such as Age Concern and the Alzheimer's Society and by means of the increased media interest in provision of services. Debates about the funding and means testing of services, provision of treatment for Alzheimer's disease and care to promote independent living are just some of the issues which are receiving attention from policy makers and the public via the media.

Service development relating to health and social care of the older person is therefore a central issue, from both a direct care context and managerial perspective. In order to achieve effective services, there needs to be an understanding of the needs of the older person and critical thinking tools can be used to initiate this process.

Thinking critically about care of the older person

Several critical thinking approaches will be used in this section to analyse the case study above. The intention is to provide a guide to the application of theory concerning an issue, rather than to offer a detailed analysis.

Moral reasoning

One fundamental issue, debated in respect of care of the older person, concerns whether or not health and social care is inherently ageist. This is clearly a moral issue, but not one that is as straightforward as it is often perceived. The debate about ageism in health and social care must of necessity explore rationing of services and resources, quality of life and futility, as well as the more obvious topics of autonomy, justice and rights. Ethical debates about access to care for older people have a tendency to be based on rather emotive arguments and not on true moral reasoning.

Some argue that ageist policy is a legitimate means of rationing limited resources and that those with their life ahead of them are necessarily more deserving of treatment; others argue that justice requires equity of access, irrespective of age or other characteristics, and that it is everyone's right to have treatment, as determined by clinical need rather than offset against potential years of life remaining. As with many moral issues, it is rarely as simple as any of these arguments and often each case, when considered in isolation, raises its own issues and each service creates different moral debates. Service development should be underpinned by consideration of key ethical issues and moral reasoning is therefore a particularly useful tool to use when planning new services or reconfiguring existing ones. Moral reasoning can also be useful in exploring the wider aspects of care of the older person such as carer support.

Chaos and complexity

Older people, like all citizens, are part of complex systems and the way they live is changing at a pace. Recent changes in society have had an impact on older people, not least that 'old age' lasts longer now, with the traditional view of 'three score years and ten' having little contemporary meaning. For many families, older people are the central support in respect of looking after children when parents are working; for some older people, social exclusion is a reality, due to the lack of extended families, poverty and fear of crime. Small changes to service provision, in social care in particular, can have a wide-ranging impact on older people and, as a critical thinking tool, chaos and complexity can therefore be of real use in analysing the needs of this particular group of service users.

Political and ideological perspectives

Ideology plays a considerable role in the social construction of older people and can therefore be of value in analysing health and social care needs, as understanding the way older people are perceived and constructed, can be valuable in determining how to use resources and deliver appropriate services. From a local political perspective, older people can be an important element of the electorate and this is becoming more evident with recent demographic changes; therefore, the overall political view of their construction is changing and consideration of this reconfiguration may be an important aspect of future service development.

Application to other areas of health and social care

This case study uses the older person as an example, however it could relate to any area of care which requires service development or redesign to meet needs. It also considers the notion of service user involvement which is a central UK policy issue, as part of making services more patient/client centred and transparent.

Chapter summary

This chapter has demonstrated how some of the critical thinking tools discussed in this book can be used to analyse practice-based issues. The examples offered, whilst having clear relevance to the specific area of care identified, also have some resonance for the wider field of health and social care thinking and practice.

Case study 1: references

Beauchamp, T. L. and Childress, J. F. (2001) *Principles of Biomedical Ethics.* 5th edition, New York: Oxford University Press.

Colwell, B. and Wainwright, D. (1981) *Behind the Blue Door: The History of the Royal College of Midwives 1881–1981.* London: Tindall.

Department of Health (1993) *Changing Childbirth: Report of the Expert Maternity Group.* London: Department of Health.

Gillon, R. (2003) 'Ethics needs principles – four can encompass the rest – and respect for autonomy should be "first among equals" ', *Journal of Medical Ethics,* 29: 307–312.

Oakley, A. (1984) *The Captured Womb: A History of the Medical Care of Pregnant Women*. Oxford: Blackwell.

Robinson, S. (1990) 'Maintaining the independence of the midwifery profession: a continuing struggle', in J. Garcia, R. Kilpatrick and M. Richards (eds), *The Politics of Maternity Care: Services for Childbearing Women in the Twentieth Century*. Oxford: Clarendon Press.

Case study 2: references

Beattie, A. (1995) 'Evaluating community development projects for health: an opportunity for dialogue', *Health Education Journal*, 54: 465–472.

Chalmers, H., Tyrer, P. and Aggleton, P. (2004) 'Personal, Social and Health Education (PSHE) Certification Programme for Community Nurses'. Evaluation of the pilot programme (Phase One), London: Thomas Coram Research Unit. Available at: www.wiredforhealth.gov.uk

Department for Education and Employment (DfEE) (1999) 'National Healthy School Standard Guidance'. Available at: www.wiredforhealth.gov.uk

Department for Education and Skills (DfES) (2001) *Schools: Achieving Success*. Department for Education and Skills: London.

Department for Education and Skills (DfES) and Department of Health (DOH) (2004) 'Guidance for Healthy School Coordinators'. Available at: www.wiredforhealth.gov.uk

Department for Education and Skills (DfES) and Department of Health (DOH) (2005) 'National Healthy School Status: A Guide for Schools'. Available at: www.wiredforhealth.gov.uk

Department of Health (DOH) (1999) *Saving Lives: Our Healthier Nation*. London: Department of Health.

Department of Health (DOH) (2004) *Choosing Health: Making Healthier Choices easier*. London: Department of Health.

Evans, D. (2004) 'Shifting the balance of power? UK public health policy and capacity building', *Critical Public Health*, 14 (1): 63–75.

Health Development Agency (HDA) (2004) *National Healthy School Standard and Local Strategic Partnership: Working Together*. London: HDA.

Morrison, M., Harrison, J., Kitson, N. and Wortley, A. (2002) 'Joined-up thinking in theory and practice: the case of healthy schools', *The Curriculum Journal*, 13 (3): 313–337.

Taylor, I. (1997) *Developing Learning in Professional Education: Partnerships for Practice*. Buckingham: Society for Research into Higher Education and the Open University.

Case study 3: references

Department of Health (DOH) (2001) *National Service Framework for Older People*. London: DOH.

King's Fund (2006) *Wanless Social Care Review Report*. London: King's Fund.

12

THE IMPLICATIONS FOR PRACTICE

Liz Smith and Julie Dickinson

This chapter will critically discuss the opportunities and challenges of critical thinking in health and social care. Consideration will also be given to the identification of learning needs to assist the reader with the formulation of a professional development plan for enhancing their critical thinking skills. Finally there will be some discussion of the promotion of critical thinking in health and social care.

Chapter aim

- To promote the application of selected critical thinking tools to health and social care practice

Learning outcomes

After studying this chapter, you should be able to:

- recognise the opportunities and challenges of applying critical thinking tools to your own practice
- identify your learning and development needs
- formulate a personal, professional development plan
- develop an action plan to promote the use of critical thinking in practice

The opportunities and challenges of applying critical thinking tools in practice

The previous chapter demonstrated how critical thinking tools can be applied to health and social care issues. This section will critically examine the opportunities in the application of critical thinking to practice.

Practice in this context is not restricted to clinical or 'coal face' type of practice but any aspect of health and social care the reader may function within, for example management and/or leadership. Particular policy issues may be alluded to within this section, however, these are for illustrative purposes only as it is recognised that policy is a constantly changing aspect of health and social care. Therefore every attempt will be made to consider the wider and more constant agendas practitioners have to address where possible.

It is a reality in health and social care that demand always appears to outstrip resources and capability to meet expectations. It is vital therefore that practitioners from all aspects of the service are both responsive to public need and expectations and demonstrate the ability to develop creative and practical solutions to the demands placed on their aspect of health and social care. There is a school of thought that creative thinking is separate and different from critical thinking however it can also be argued that they are each complimentary to the other (Daly, 1998). This can be particularly so in health and social care where policy is set by the Government whilst practitioners are required to translate the principles of the policies into the realities of service delivery. Creative solutions to the apparent mismatch between policy and service delivery can arguably only be achieved if critical thinking is applied to both the aims and objectives of the policy and to the problems which require solutions. It is appropriate therefore for both clinicians and managers to utilise critical thinking approaches to effectively implement policy into practice. This can be seen as a challenge as it is perceived that modern health and social care organisations are not supportive of critical thinkers. However this may be because the link between critical and creative thinking has not always been recognised and the language used by critical thinking textbooks is not easy to understand. Critical thinking needs to be constructive rather than merely analytical to ensure that in 'unpacking' the issues and attempting to make sense of them from whatever approach is seen as relevant and that there is a practical point to the exercise. The 'so what' question needs to be addressed to ensure that there is real meaning to service delivery. Critical thinking is therefore central to decision-making and problem-solving in health and social care.

Theorists discuss two types of decision-making: rational and phenomenological (Harbison, 1991). The rational approach to decision-making being where the practitioner analyses the situation and makes a judgement which is rational and logical, he/she can then be explicit about the knowledge and judgement underpinning the decision. This type of decision-making can be applied to practice-based decision-making related to client care, to policy implementation or to management problems.

The analysis of the situation can be improved significantly if critical thinking is applied to the process, indeed it could be argued that it is essential that this occurs to limit the possibilities of inappropriate actions being taken. For example, a practitioner who considers the situation of an elderly person with dementia could apply moral reasoning or critical realism to determine what is the best course of action to maintain the balance between care and independence; a manager could apply feminist thinking to a problem with skill mix and resources or a practitioner could use knowledge of political ideology to make a case for a change in service delivery.

In addition, practitioners within health and social care settings are required to be non-judgemental in their approach to patients/clients and their families. However, objectivity can be difficult when faced with a child-protection scenario or an abusive patient/client or a dying cancer sufferer. Critical thinking tools can be an aid to practitioners in putting aside their own views and values and consider the situation less subjectively.

Seymour, Kinn and Sutherland (2003) argue that there is a danger in applying critical thinking alone to problem-solving and reasoning as personal attributes and the working environment will and should influence the context of thinking. However whilst this may be true it is also true that whether decision-making is in relation to a patient/client situation or to organisational strategy it is important to recognise and sometimes filter out the influences of personal values and the working environment. This is arguably best achieved by taking a critical thinking approach where all information is considered from a more analytical and objective perspective. That is not to imply that subjectivity be ignored entirely however it is essential that practitioners recognise and evaluate all the influences on their decision-making. There is a danger that practitioners can make assumptions about a situation if this does not occur. Consider, for example, the nurse who decides to administer an unfamiliar drug without checking the dosage or contraindications because she believes the doctor will have the knowledge and skills necessary for safe prescribing. She may be right and the consequences of administration of the drug may be entirely positive however she may not and the patient may be overdosed. The knowledge and skills of the doctor are an assumption on her part and she has not thoroughly considered the issue of her accountability in administering a drug she knows little or nothing about. This is perhaps a simplistic example of how critical thinking can be used in day-to-day practice; nonetheless it is illustrative of how important critically thinking and not making assumptions or value judgments is to the safety and quality of care delivery.

Activity

Reflect on decisions you have made at work recently.

- How much influence did your personal values and the working environment have on the decision?
- Would the decision have been different if you had utilised a critical thinking approach?
- Would you have come to the same decision but felt that the process was more thorough?

The second approach to decision-making is phenomenological or intuitive (Harbison, 1991). It could be suggested that if intuition is a feature of this decision-making process, critical thinking has no part of it, indeed it has been argued that intuitive decision-making should not be a part of health and social care practice (English, 1993) because it is not a 'scientific' approach. However Benner (1985) makes strong links between expert knowledge and intuition and it could therefore be argued that critical thinking is instrumental in acquiring expertise and is therefore relevant to phenomenological decision-making. One attribute that is generally associated with expert practice is that of reflection and, as is discussed later in this chapter, reflection should be a critical process (Paul and Heaslip, 1995). Indeed some of the criticisms of reflection levelled on the basis of Foucault's concepts of power-knowledge (Cotton, 2001; Gilbert, 2001) could perhaps be answered if a more critical approach to reflective practice is adopted since it would not confine them to instrumental ways of practice and institutionalised thinking as Cotton (2001) suggests.

Critical thinking can also be useful in determining whether or not the intuitive interpretation of a situation is of use since both the expert experiencing the intuition or 'gut feeling' and those working with him/her will need to determine the action required in response to it (Paul and Heaslip, 1995). There is a prevailing philosophy within health and social care that practice should be evidence based. Along with this there has been a proliferation in guidelines and protocols to provide the practitioner with a 'recipe' for best practice. The challenge for the critical thinker is to navigate their way through the evidence and make sense of it in a way which allows for effective practice which is also appropriate for the situation. The emphasis has been on the more scientific evidence which does not always acknowledge the qualitative and holistic nature of health and social care.

It is also true that scientific evidence does not always deliver certainty and that critical thinking is therefore necessary to assess the evidence available and utilise it as effectively as possible. It may be that practitioners perceive that the policy of evidence-based practice does not encourage critical thinking which may lead to a rejection of 'best practice' in a given situation however the concept of guidelines rather than policy is to allow for practitioners to use their knowledge and experience to provide quality care which best meets the needs of the patient/client. It is also true that if no-one ever questioned the appropriateness of a practice the evidence would never develop and practice would become stagnated and ritualistic rather than innovative and dynamic. Risk taking has to be part of health and social care practice however critical thinking should enable the practitioner to assess the risk to ensure that it is minimised and managed whilst changes are evaluated.

Critical thinking can also be closely linked with leadership in health and social care. Leadership in health and social care is often very much related to developing a 'vision' for the future and managing change. There is much discussion around whether leaders should be transactional or transformational in health and social care. Transactional leadership is perceived as being 'managerial' as it involves an emphasis on getting the job done and a reward/punishment approach to followers. Transformational leadership, by contrast, is related to inspiring people to follow the 'vision'. Developing a vision for services, whether at a team or organisational level, also requires critical thinking as there is a need for the vision to fit with the 'bigger picture' or what Mintzberg (1992) describes as the 'helicopter' view.

There is also a need for the effective leader to pay attention to detail; it is insufficient to communicate the 'bigger picture', as knowledge and understanding of service delivery and of the key stakeholders is important in creating a realistic and achievable vision (Milner and Joyce, 2005). Critical thinking can be crucial in assisting with determining the relevant detail allowing the leader to put aside the irrelevant. Hersey and Blanchard (1988) suggest that effective leaders adapt their style to the situation and the needs of their followers. It could be argued that in order to adapt to the situation an effective leader has to be able to think critically about it and the needs of their followers.

Activity

Consider an idea or vision you may have for the services you are involved in.

- How may any of the critical thinking tools discussed in this book assist with ascertaining the detail required to ensure that your idea is feasible?

Management of change remains very much informed by the work of social scientist Kurt Lewin (Burnes, 2004). Despite some contemporary criticism Lewin's work is considered to be the basis of more modern theories on change management. Lewin argued that there are two requirements for success in relation to behavioural change:

- to analyse and understand the formation and motivation of social groupings (field theory and group dynamics)
- to change the behaviour of social groups (action research and 3-step model of change)

Critical thinking can be useful in both these elements of change management as there are tools which lend themselves to the analysis of group behaviours and interactions (e.g. chaos and complexity, feminism) and also to the critical appraisal of information and evidence applicable to the proposed change.

Critical thinking can therefore be applied at all levels and areas of health and social care. It has uses both in respect of patient/client care, practice development and leadership and management of services. It can be utilised to enhance the decision-making of practitioners and thereby improve the quality of care delivery. The current agendas of inter-professional team working and public involvement in service development can be facilitated by a more critical approach to strategic thinking and change management as critical thinking can enhance understanding of individual, group and organisational behaviours. At the very least critical thinking should encourage a more objective and measured approach to care which is entirely congruent with the need to be accountable and transparent in respect of care and service delivery. Opportunities are abundant; the challenge is to develop the skills and understanding to access them.

Continuing Professional Development (CPD) in health and social care

One major area where the development and use of critical thinking skills is essential is in CPD. The importance of CPD for health and social workers cannot be underestimated and supports the ideology of clinical governance and the implementation of evidence-based practice, and is championed by Government, professional organisations and practitioners alike. According to Alsop (2000), CPD is: 'a term commonly used to denote the process of ongoing education and development of health care professionals, from initial qualifying education and for the duration of professional life, in order to maintain competence to practice and increase professional proficiency and expertise' (p. 1). This definition implies that CPD is both an obligation and a privilege and is only associated with professional groups. For the purpose of this chapter, CPD is seen as related to 'practice' and therefore should encompass all health and social care workers.

The development of all health and social care staff is a fundamental aim of the NHS Plan (DOH 2000). There is not only an expectation that all staff should keep their knowledge and skills up to date, but that significant resources were allocated to CPD. This was followed up by more detailed policy statements in 2001 with 'Working Together – Learning Together' (DOH 2001) which provided a framework for this development around the concept of life-long learning for staff to be: 'Equipped with the skills and knowledge to work flexibly in support of patients; supported to grow, develop and realize their potential' (p. 8). This document is particularly relevant to exploring the link between CPD and critical thinking as it cites core skills of 'understanding', 'seeking out' and 'recognition' all of which can be associated with being a critical thinker. A main element of this policy is the 'Knowledge and Skills Escalator' which defines and describes the knowledge and skills NHS staff need to apply in their work to deliver quality services. CPD policy specifically in relation to social care is not as clear, however, policy focuses more on actual service need such as 'Adult Services' or 'Elderly Care' rather than considering the care sector as a whole. It could be argued that this could be due largely to the many service providers involved.

At present the main national organisations who lead the development and training of health and social care staff are 'Skills for Care' (www.skillsforcare.org.uk) and 'Skills for Health' (www.skillsforhealth.org.uk) fairly new organisations who come under the umbrella of the UK 'Sector Skills Councils'. Their role is to facilitate the education needed for health and social care delivery. In addition there are the regulatory bodies associated with health and social care staff who have some responsibility for ensuring those registered with them maintain their knowledge and skills. The Nursing and Midwifery Council (NMC) and the Health Professions' Council (HPC) specifically have a requirement for a portfolio of evidence of CPD to be maintained for all registrants. Critical thinking is not specified as an essential element of these portfolios, however, since the work should not simply be a collection of certificates but a reflection on learning and development it is arguably an implicit requirement.

As discussed earlier, CPD for non-professional groups is seen as a policy requirement however it is not yet well organised. The National Occupational Standards appear to be the main focus for the development of health and social care staff but there seems to be no agreement on how they are developed, implemented or assessed. The Sector Skills Councils mentioned above, see this as a major way forward, but as yet implementation has been at local rather than national level and is therefore dependent on local resources and enthusiasm rather than a national agenda.

Although not recognised as a profession the 'Society of Health Education and Health Promotion Specialists (SHEPS)', which represents some Health Promotion and Public Health Specialists, has developed its own voluntary register with framework of standards relating to knowledge and practice (SHEPS, 2006). It's approach does suggest however a possible dilemma in the use of critical thinking skills alongside the production of standards needed to register as a profession.

Activity

List the CPD activity you have done in the last year and consider the following:

- Why did you choose these particular activities?
- Did the activities encourage the use of critical thinking skills?
- In what way is CPD encouraged in your current work environment?

Portfolio development and critical thinking

Portfolios can be useful in many ways as discussed by Baume (2003). At their simplest they are used as a repository of materials describing an experience, topic or course. Leading on from this they can be used for assessment purposes to provide the evidence needed to fulfil the requirements of a programme of study and, as discussed earlier, for registration purposes. At its most rewarding and challenging a portfolio can be used to aid development, and this is where critical thinking skills can be invaluable.

The components of a portfolio will of course reflect its use, but will also be guided in health and social care by the nature of the associated role. Examples from the literature (Alsop, 2002; Lawler and Wells, 1999; Stewart, 1998) tend to agree on the approaches needed to produce the portfolio but shy away from being prescriptive on the content needed. This approach is also promoted by Baume (2003) who presents a list of 'Elements' to help guide the development. These include very practical elements such as having a clear structure with a clear index or search function (virtual portfolios are becoming more popular) and incorporating evidence of achievement which may be mapped to standards or learning outcomes. Most importantly though, and a clear link with critical thinking, is the importance of the use of what he calls critical reflection, an opportunity to step back from the evidence and analyse its relevance in terms of developing knowledge and skills. Alsop (2002) promotes its importance for occupational therapists and questions whether the use of reflective practice, now a common term in health and social care practice, fully takes into account the critical element which enables personal and professional growth.

Using critical reflection as a tool can be of benefit to many practitioners and does not need to be focused on a particular profession. In all forms of reflection there needs to be an experience to reflect upon. This is sometimes defined as a 'critical incident' (Lawler and Wells, 1999), although the use of the word 'critical' is this context can suggest that the incident in some way has to be special and is often interpreted as being a negative experience, however, some of the most beneficial learning can be done in reflecting on day-to-day practice but in a critical way. Reflections on the experience need to be behaviourally, cognitively and normatively assessed and should involve how the practitioner and others reacted, analysing why this may be, evaluating the experience as a learning opportunity and synthesising all the information to inform practice.

Activity

- Consider an experience in practice that could provide a learning opportunity. Reflect on the activity (Behaviourally – what was done? Cognitively – thoughts on the activity, Normatively – your feelings, or those expressed by others)
- Using one or more relevant approaches to critical thinking explored in previous chapters, critically analyse what happened and evaluate your practice
- Synthesise the experience with your analysis and conclude of what you have learnt in the process
- Relate this learning to how this could improve similar experiences in practice

---

Personal, professional development planning

Personal, professional development plans are an ideal way of taking responsibility for and managing the developmental process necessary to become a critical thinker. Such plans are also in keeping with the ethos of life-long learning; a central element of quality health and social care practice. Martin (2006) offers a five-stage model for personal development which can be applied to attaining knowledge and skills in relation to critical thinking.

- Stage 1: Reflection
- Stage 2: Planning
- Stage 3: Recording
- Stage 4: Taking Action
- Stage 5: Reviewing

Stage 1 of the model should help to not only identify the skills and knowledge required but should also be about reflecting on the knowledge and skills already acquired. It may be useful to utilise a tool such as SWOT analysis (strengths, weaknesses, opportunities and threats) to encourage consideration of the positives as well as the gaps in knowledge and skills. Stage 2 should encourage a consideration of short- and long-term goals and the resources available. The obvious sources of critical thinking skills are courses and literature; however, it is worth thinking about those people you perceive to be critical thinkers and whether they can offer anything in relation to your development in a formal or informal way. Recording a plan of action is not essential but does encourage some to carry out their intent and at the very least can sometimes be an aid to a more structured approach to development. Martin (2006) offers headings; however, it is often more appropriate to take a more personalised approach to the plan and determine headings which best meet your own needs. Development will not occur without action and it is appropriate to critical thinking to review and evaluate progress.

Chapter summary

This chapter has highlighted some of the applications of critical thinking in respect of health and social care. This has consequently signposted some of the opportunities and challenges facing critical thinkers in health and social care whether at care delivery, leadership or management level. Links have been identified with decision-making, reflection and personal, professional development and guidance offered in relation to planning for personal development to aid with the attainment of appropriate knowledge and skills in critical thinking.

Sources of further reading and exploration

Books and journals

Alsop, A. (2000) *Continuing Professional Development: A Guide for Therapists.* Oxford: Blackwell Publishing.

Baume, D. (2003) *LTSN Generic Centre Continuing Professional Development Series No. 3 Supporting Portfolio Development.* York: Learning and Teaching Support Network.

Milner, E. and Joyce, P. (2005) *Lessons in Leadership: Meeting the Challenges of Public Services Management.* Abingdon: Routledge.

Paul, R. W. and Heaslip, P. (1995) 'Critical thinking and intuitive nursing practice', *Journal of Advanced Nursing*, 22: 40–47.

Stewart, S (1998) 'The place of portfolios within continuing professional development', *British Journal of Therapy and Rehabilitation*, March 1998 (5): 5.

SUMMARY

Stella Jones-Devitt and Liz Smith

The three sections of this book, comprising theoretical overview, key tools and application to health and social care, are all premised on the present context for health and social care. The pace of change in health and social care is fuelled by the shifting dynamics of a range of policy drivers; yet there is a level of predictability – even within the critical uncertainty of future practice – that this book has highlighted. Such predictabilities can be grouped into three discrete areas: the future of health and social care provision; the ascendancy of neoliberalism (and the resultant individualism); the potential impact on practitioner skills.

The future of health and social care provision

The twenty-first century has shifted the debate away from that of public–private tensions, to one in which 'Third Way' models of social justice or 'Third Sector' engagement (as it is increasingly called) is becoming de rigueur for public services. The official website for the Office of Government Commerce (2006) describes the Third Sector as: 'a range of institutions, which occupy the space between the State and private sector'; these not-for-profit agencies offer what was once deemed unthinkable: they provide mainstream public services *instead of* state-run provision, rather than *in addition* to existing arrangements. This exemplifies the clear political will to diversify funding arrangements for sustaining health and social care provision.

As alluded to in later chapters of this book, the commissioning of health and social care services is moving towards ever-reducing state funding, alongside the planned reduction of direct state involvement in a range of public services. As highlighted in several chapters, the resonance of this approach for existing practitioners will involve greater blurring of professional boundaries, resulting in emergence of new worker roles, alongside a re-definition of established profession-specific approaches; key exemplars include the creation of multi-sectoral 'Children's Services' and 'Rehabilitation Services' departments.

The continued lessening of self-regulation by individual professional bodies is a further testament to the political momentum for public sector efficiencies and greater accountability. The commissioning of the landmark Gershon Report (2004) mapped out the cross-cutting efficiency measures the state should undertake, recognising the growing relationship with the Third Sector. It removed the key assumption that public services should always be delivered by public sector organisations, stating that one of the key recommendations should involve: 'considering carefully the appropriate assignment of risk between the statutory body and the voluntary and community organisation when contracting for service provision' (p. 34).

Ascendancy of neoliberalism

This escalating cultural drift, into accepting inevitable fragmentation and devolution of mainstream public services, mirrors wider neoliberal global economic drivers. Recent events within the health and social care sector provide perfect exemplars of underpinning neoliberal concepts, identified by Olsen and Peters (2005) as comprising: a world of global choice for individuals, organisations and multinational corporations, characterised by regulation via some of the 'softer' free trade principles, alongside minimal or non-existent state interference.

This is also characterised by the resultant shift away from positioning the individual as passive client or patient, to one in which seductive notions of 'active consumer' prevail. Implications for the health and social care practitioner are well documented within this book: Hunter and Marks (2005) described how many front-line staff perceive that this has resulted in increased target-setting rather than visionary leadership; Checkland (2004) pointed out the misnomer of 'client' or 'patient' evolving into an active 'consumer', suggesting that they have little real choice in accessing key services. This paradox often leaves the practitioner in a state of suspended animation that challenges the most critical of thinkers: they must act as autonomous, multi-skilled inter-sectoral workers, whilst operating within increasingly audited and externally limiting frameworks.

Impact on practitioner skills

The practitioner needs to be able to make sense of the pace of change within the health and social care domain, alongside the ensuing fragmentation. This book has illustrated that in order to survive and 'thrive' in the present climate, practitioners need to develop an understanding of key ideological drivers for policy provision and change, whilst thinking very critically about mechanisms that can help reconnect and locate their practice in this evolving context.

To make connections between the fast-moving policy drivers and everyday health and social care practice, practitioners need to be sanguine about dealing with chaos and change; hence, our Chapter 1 definition of critical thinking prevails, concerning the skills needed to make sense of the world by questioning the questions, challenging assumptions, and by recognising that bodies of knowledge can be chaotic and evolving. Only then will the health and social care practitioner be able to deal effectively with the enduring critical uncertainties, and be able to continually improve their thinking, in order to influence both present-day service provision and future policy and practice.

REFERENCES

Acheson, D. (1989) *Independent Inquiry into Inequalities in Health Report*. London: HMSO.

Alcock, C., Payne, S. and Sullivan, M. (2000) *Introducing Social Policy*. Harlow: Prentice Hall.

Allsop, J., Jones, K. and Baggott, R. (2004) 'Health consumer groups in the UK: a new social movement?' *Sociology of Health and Illness*, 26 (6): 737–756.

Almond, B. (1998) *Exploring Ethics: A Traveller's Tale*. Oxford: Blackwell.

Alsop, A. (2000) *Continuing Professional Development: A Guide for Therapists*. Oxford: Blackwell Publishing.

Alvesson, M. (2002) *Postmodernism and Social Research*. Buckingham: Open University Press.

Alvesson, M. and Skoldberg, K. (2000) *Reflexive Methodology: New Vistas for Qualitative Research*. London: Sage.

Antonovsky, A. (1987) *Unravelling the Mystery of Health: How People Manage Others and Stay Well*. New York: Wiley.

Appignanesi, R. and Garratt, C. (1999) *Introducing Postmodernism*. Duxford: Icon Books.

Archer, M. (1995) *Realist Social Theory: The Morphogenetic Approach*. Cambridge: Cambridge University Press.

Archer, M., Bhaskar, R., Lawson, T. and Norrie, A. (eds) (1998) *Critical Realism: Essential Readings*. London: Routledge.

Arney, W. R. and Bergen, B. J. (1984) *Medicine and the Management of Living: Taming the Last Great Beast*. Chicago, IL: University of Chicago Press.

Bacon, F. (1605) *The Advancement of Learning*. Online version available at: www.classic-literature.co.uk/british-authors/16th-century/francis-bacon/the-advancement-of-learning/

Bacon, F. (1620) in L. Jardine and M. Silverthorne (eds) (2000) *Francis Bacon: The New Organon*. Cambridge: Cambridge University Press.

Banks, S. (2004) *Ethics, Accountability and the Social Professions*. Basingstoke: Palgrave Macmillan.

Barnett, R. (1997) *Higher Education: A Critical Business*. Buckingham: The Society for Research into Higher Education and the Open University.

Barr, R. (1993) in G. Siann (1994) *Gender, Sex and Sexuality: Contemporary Psychological Perspectives*. London: Taylor and Francis.

Barry, N. (2000) *Introduction to Modern Political Theory*. Basingstoke: Palgrave Macmillan.

Baume, D. (2003) *LTSN Generic Centre Continuing Professional Development Series No. 3 Supporting Portfolio Development*. York: Learning and Teaching Support Network.

Beattie, A. (1995) 'Evaluating community development projects for health: an opportunity for dialogue', *Health Education Journal*, 54: 465–472.

Beauchamp, T. L. (2003) 'Methods and principles in biomedical ethics', *Journal of Medical Ethics*, 29: 269–274.

Beauchamp, T. L. and Childress, J. F. (2001) *Principles of Biomedical Ethics* (5th edition). New York: Oxford University Press.

Beck, U. and Beck-Gernsheim, E. (2003) *Individualization: Institutionalized Individualism and Its Social and Political Consequences*. London, Thousand Oaks and New Delhi: Sage Publications.

Becker, P. E. (2000) 'Boundaries and silences in a post-feminist sociology', *Sociology of Religion*, 61 (4): 399–408.

Bendelow, G., Carpenter, M., Vautier, C. and Williams, S. (eds) (2001) *Gender, Health and Healing: The Public/Private Divide*. London: Routledge.

Benn, P. (1998) *Ethics*. London: Routledge.

Benner, P. (1985) *From Novice to Expert: Excellence and Power in Clinical Nursing Practice*. San Francisco, CA: Addison-Wesley.

Berman, S. (2001) 'Opening the closed mind: making assumptions, jumping to conclusions', *Etc.*, 58 (4): 429–439.

Bhaskar, R. (1979) *The Possibility of Naturalism: A Philosophical Critique of the Contemporary Human Sciences*. Brighton: Harvester.

Black, S. E. and Lynch, L. M. (2001) in W. W. Powell and K. Snellman (2004) 'The knowledge economy', *Annual Review of Sociology*, 30: 199–220.

Blackler, F. (1995) 'Knowledge, knowledge work and organizations: an overview and interpretation', *Organization Studies*, 16 (6): 1021–1046.

Bordo, S. (1995) *Unbearable Weight: Feminism, Western Culture and the Body*. Berkeley and Los Angeles, CA: University of California Press.

Boychuk Duchscher, J. E. (1999) 'Catching the wave: understanding the concept of critical thinking', *Journal of Advanced Nursing*, 29 (3): 577–584.

Brookfield, S. D. (1987) *Developing Critical Thinkers: Challenging Adults to Explore Alternative Ways of Thinking and Acting*. San Francisco, CA: Jossey-Bass.

Brown, B., Crawford, P. and Hicks, C. (2003) *Evidence-based Research*. London: Open University Press.

Brown, J. S. and Duguid, P. (1991) 'Organizational learning and communities of practice: towards a unified view of working, learning and innovation', *Organizational Science*, 2 (1): 40–57.

Burgess, H. (2004) 'Redesigning the curriculum for social work education: complexity, conformity, chaos, creativity, collaboration?' *Social Work Education*, 23 (2): 163–183.

Burnes, B. (2004) *Managing Change*. Harlow: Prentice Hall.

Burrell, G. and Morgan, G. (1979) *Sociological Paradigms and Organizational Analysis*. London: Heinemann Educational Books.

Burton-Jones, A. (1999) *Knowledge Capitalism: Business, Work and Learning in the New Economy*. Oxford: Oxford University Press.

Callinicos, A. T. (2001) *Against the Third Way*. Cambridge: Polity Press.

Callinicos, A. T. (2003) *The New Mandarins of American Power*. Cambridge: Polity Press.

Campbell, A., Gillett, G. and Jones, G. (2005) *Medical Ethics* (4th edition). Melbourne: Oxford University Press.

Capra, F. (1983) *The Turning Point*. London: Flamingo Books.

Carter, B. (1994) *Child and Infant Pain*. London: Chapman & Hall.

Chalmers, H., Tyrer, P. and Aggleton, P. (2004) 'Personal, social and health education (PSHE) certification programme for community nurses', *Evaluation of the pilot programme (Phase One)*. London: Thomas Coram Research Unit. Available at: www.wiredforhealth.gov.uk

Checkland, K. (2004) 'National service frameworks and UK general practitioners: street-level bureaucrats at work?' *Sociology of Health and Illness*, 26 (7): 951–971.

Cheek, J. (2000) *Postmodern and poststructural approaches to nursing research*. Thousand Oaks, CA: Sage.

Chomsky, N. (1989) *Necessary Illusions: Thought Control in Democratic Societies*. London: Pluto.

Cotton, A. H. (2001) 'Private thoughts in public spheres: issues in reflection and reflective practices in nursing', *Journal of Advanced Nursing*, 36 (4): 512–519.

Colwell, B. and Wainwright, D. (1981) *Behind the Blue Door: The History of the Royal College of Midwives 1881–1981*. London: Bailliere Tindall.

Cottrell, S. (2005) *Critical Thinking Skills: Developing Effective Analysis and Argument*. Basingstoke: Palgrave Macmillan.

Creek, J. (1997) 'The truth is no longer out there', *British Journal of Occupational Therapy*, 60 (2): 50–52.

Curry, J. (1997) 'The dialectic of knowledge-in-production: value creation in late capitalism and the rise of knowledge-centered production', *Electronic Journal of Sociology*, 2 (3). Available at:http://epe.lac-bac.gc.ca/100/201/300/ejofsociology/1999/991102/content/vol002.003/curry.html

Daly, W. M. (1998) 'Critical thinking as an outcome of nursing education. What is it? Why is it important to nursing practice?' *Journal of Advanced Nursing*, 28 (2): 323–331.

Dalziel, Y. (2003) 'The role of nurses in public health' in A. Watterson, *Public Health in Practice*. Basingstoke: Palgrave Macmillan.

Davies, C. (2002) 'What about the girl next door? Gender and the politics of professional self-regulation' in G. Bendelow, M. Carpenter, C. Vautier and S. Williams, *Gender, Health and Healing: The Public/Private Divide*. London: Routledge.

Daykin, N. (2001) 'Sociology' in J. Naidoo and J. Wills, *Health Studies: An Introduction*. Basingstoke: Palgrave.

de Groot, J. and Maynard, M. (1993) 'Facing the 1990s: Problems and possibilities for women's studies' in J. de Groot and M. Maynard (eds) *Women's Studies in the 1990s: Doing Things Differently?* Basingstoke: Macmillan Press.

Dekel, R., Solomon, Z., Elkit, A. and Ginzburg, K. (2004) 'World assumptions and combat-related posttraumatic stress disorder', *Journal of Social Psychology*, 144 (4): 407–420.

Department for Education and Employment (DfEE) (1999) *National Healthy School Standard Guidance*. Available at: www.wiredforhealth.gov.uk

Department for Education and Skills (DfES) (2001) *Schools: Achieving Success*. London: Department for Education and Skills.

Department for Education and Skills (DfES) and Department of Health (DOH) (2004) 'Guidance for Healthy School Coordinators'. Available at: www.wiredforhealth.gov.uk

Department for Education and Skills (DfES) and Department of Health (DOH) (2005) *National Healthy School Status: A Guide for Schools*. Available at: www.wiredforhealth.gov.uk

Department of Health (DOH) (1993) *Changing Childbirth: Report of the Expert Maternity Group*. London: Department of Health.

Department of Health (DOH) (1999) *Saving lives: Our Healthier Nation.* London: Department of Health.

Department of Health (DOH) (2000) *Coronary Heart Disease: National Service Framework – Modern Standards and Service Models.* London: Department of Health.

Department of Health (DOH) (2000) *The NHS Plan: A Plan for Investment, a Plan for Reform.* London: Department of Health.

Department of Health (DOH) (2001) *National Service Framework for Older People.* London: Department of Health.

Department of Health (DOH) (2002) *Liberating the Talents: Helping Primary Care Trusts and Nurses to Deliver the NHS Plan.* London: Department of Health.

Department of Health (DOH) (2004) *Choosing Health: Making Healthier Choices easier.* London: Department of Health.

Department of Health and Social Security (1980) *The Black Report on Inequalities in Health.* London: HMSO.

Derrida, J. (1974) *Of Grammatology.* Translated by G. C. Spivak. Baltimore, MD: John Hopkins University Press.

Derrida, J. (2001) *Writing and Difference.* London: Routledge Classics.

Descartes, R. (1628) *Rules for the Direction of the Mind.* Online version available at: http://faculty.uccb.ns.ca/philosophy/kbryson/rulesfor.htm

Dickinson, J. and Jones-Devitt, S. (2003) 'Health-promoting practice' in D. Palmer and S. Kaur (eds) *Core Skills for Nurse Practitioners.* London: Whurr Publishers.

Doyal, L. (2002) 'Gender equity in health: debates and dilemmas' in G. Bendelow, M. Carpenter, C. Vautier and S. Williams, *Gender, Health and Healing: The Public/Private Divide.* London: Routledge.

Drucker, P. F. (1993) *Post-Capitalist Society.* New York: Harper Business.

Edwards, R. and Usher, R. (2001) 'Lifelong learning: a postmodern condition of education?' *Adult Education Quarterly,* 51 (4): 273–287.

Ehrenreich, B. (2005) 'What is socialist feminism?' *Monthly Review,* 57 (3): 70–77.

Elder, L. and Paul, R. (2002) 'Distinguishing between inferences and assumptions', *Journal of Developmental Education,* 25 (3): 34–35.

Engels, F. (1986) *The Origin of the Family, Private Property and the State.* London: Penguin Books.

English, I. (1993) 'Intuition as a function of the expert nurse: A critique of Benner's novice to expert model', *Journal of Advanced Nursing,* 18 (3): 387–393.

Ennis, R. H. (1995) *Critical Thinking.* Upper Saddle River, NJ: Prentice Hall.

Epstein, B. (2002) 'The successes and failures of feminism', *Journal of Women's History,* 14 (2): 118–25.

Etzioni, A. (1995) *The Spirit of Community: Rights, Responsibilities and the Communitarian Agenda.* London: Fontana.

Evans, D. (2004) 'Shifting the balance of power? UK public health policy and capacity building', *Critical Public Health,* 14 (1): 63–75.

Facione, N. C. and Facione, P. (1996) 'Externalizing the critical thinking in knowledge development and clinical judgement', *Nursing Outlook,* 44 (3): 129–136.

Faludi, S. (1992) *Backlash: The Undeclared War against Women.* London: Chatto and Windus.

Fenwick, T. (2001) 'Knowledge and the enterprising self: workplace refugees navigating entrepreneurial discourse', *Studies in the Education of Adults,* 3 (2): 127–134.

Fisher, A. (2001) *Critical Thinking: An introduction.* Cambridge: Cambridge University Press.

Flew, A. (1984) *A Dictionary of Philosophy*. London: Pan Books.

Foster, P. (1995) *Women and the Health Care Industry: An Unhealthy Relationship*. Milton Keynes: Open University Press.

Foucault, M. (1989) *The Birth of the Clinic: An Archaeology of Medical Perception*. London: Routledge.

Fraser, S. W. and Greenhalgh, T. (2001) 'Coping with complexity: educating for capability', *British Medical Journal*, 323: 799–803.

Freeden, M. (1996) *Ideologies and Political Theory: A Conceptual Approach*. Oxford and New York: Oxford University Press.

Fukuyama, F. (2006) *After the Neocons: Where the Right Went Wrong*. London: Profile Books Ltd.

Gadamer, H. (1975) *Truth and Method*. London: Sheed and Ward.

Gershon, P. (2004) *Releasing Resources to the Front Line: Independent Review of Public Sector Efficiency*. London: HMSO.

Giddens, A. (1976) *New Rules of Sociological Method*. London: Hutchinson.

Giddens, A. (1998) *The Third Way: The Revival of Social Democracy*. Cambridge: Polity Press.

Gilbert, T. (2001) 'Reflective practice and clinical supervision: meticulous rituals of the confessional', *Journal of Advanced Nursing*, 36 (2): 199–205.

Gilligan, C. (1993) *In a Different Voice: Psychological Theory and Women's Development*. Cambridge, MA: Harvard University Press.

Gillis, S. and Munford, R. (2004) 'Genealogies and generations: the politics and praxis of third wave feminism', *Women's History Review*, 13 (2): 165–182.

Gillon, R. (2003) 'Ethics needs principles – four can encompass the rest – and respect for autonomy should be "first among equals" ', *Journal of Medical Ethics*, 29: 307–312.

Ginzburg, K. (2004) 'PTSD and world assumptions following myocardial infarction: a longitudinal study', *American Journal of Orthopsychiatry*, 74 (3): 286–292.

Gollub, J. and Solomon, T. (1996) 'Chaos theory' in K. A. Ransom (ed.) *Academic American Encyclopaedia*, Volume 4. Danbury, CT: Grolier Inc.

Gramsci, A. (1935) in A. Heywood (2003) *Political Ideologies: An Introduction*. (3rd edition) Basingstoke: Palgrave Macmillan, pp. 8–9.

Gray, J. (2003) *Straw Dogs: Thoughts on Humans and Other Animals*. London: Granta.

Grbich, C. (1999) *Qualitative Research in Health: An Introduction*. London: Sage.

Great Britain (1998) *Human Rights Act 1998 Elisabeth II. Chapter 42*. London: HMSO.

Greer, G. (1999*) The Whole Woman*. London: Doubleday.

Hadley, R. and Clough, R. (1996) *Care in Chaos*. London: Cassel.

Hall, J. M. (1999) 'Marginalization revisited: critical, postmodern and liberation perspectives', *Advances in Nursing Science*, 22 (1): 88–102.

Halpern, D. (1989) *Thought and Knowledge: An Introduction to Critical Thinking*. Mahwah, NJ: Laurence Erlbaum Associates Inc.

Halpern, D. (1996) *Thought and Knowledge: An Introduction to Critical Thinking* (3rd edition). Mahwah, NJ: Laurence Erlbaum Associates Inc.

Hammersley, M. (1995) *The Politics of Social Research*. London, Thousand Oaks and New Delhi: Sage Publications.

Hanson, F. (2006) 'Self Care – Essentials of 21st Century Health Care Reform'. ASI Think Piece, Adam Smith Institute. Available at: www.adamsmith.org/health/index.php/tools/think_print/selfcare/

Harbison, J. (1991) 'Clinical decision making in nursing', *Journal of Advanced Nursing*, 16: 404–407.

Hardey, M. (1999) 'Doctor in the house: the Internet as a source of lay health knowledge and the challenge to expertise', *Sociology of Health and Illness*, 21 (6): 820–835.

Harris, R. (2001) in R. Alfara-Lefevre (2004) *Critical Thinking and Clinical Judgment; A Practical Approach* (3rd edition). Philadelphia: W. B. Saunders Company.

Health Development Agency (HDA) (2004) *National Healthy School Standard and Local Strategic Partnership: Working Together*. London: Health Development Agency.

Hersey, P. and Blanchard, K. H. (1988) *Management of Organizational Behaviour* (5th edition). Eaglewood Cliffs, NJ: Prentice Hall.

Heywood, A. (1998) *Political Ideologies: An Introduction* (2nd edition). Basingstoke: Palgrave Macmillan.

Heywood, A. (2003) *Political Ideologies: An Introduction* (3rd edition). Basingstoke: Palgrave Macmillan.

Heywood, A. (2004) *Political Theory: An Introduction* (3rd edition). Basingstoke: Palgrave Macmillan.

Holland, J. and Adkins, L. (eds) (1996) *Sex, Sensibility and the Gendered Body*. Basingstoke: Macmillan.

Hollows, J. (2000) *Feminism, Femininity and Popular Culture*. Manchester: Manchester University Press.

Hope, T. (2004) *Medical Ethics: A Very Short Introduction*. New York: Oxford University Press.

Houston, S. (2001) 'Transcending the fissure in risk theory: critical realism and child welfare', *Child and Family Social Work*, 6 (3): 219–228.

Howard, R. (1982) *Three Faces of Hermeneutics: An Introduction to Current Theories of Understanding*. Berkeley, CA: University of California Press.

Hugman, R. (2005) *New Approaches in Ethics for the Caring Professions*. Basingstoke: Palgrave Macmillan.

Hunter, D. and Marks, L. (2005) *Managing for Health*. London: King's Fund Publications.

Hurd, P. (2001) in R. Paul, *The State of Critical Thinking Today: The Need for a Substantive Concept of Critical Thinking*. Available at: www.criticalthinking.org/resources/articles/the-state-ct-today.shtml

Jackson, J. (2006) *Truth, Trust and Medicine*. London: Routledge.

Jaeger, S. M. (2001) 'Teaching health care ethics: the importance of moral sensitivity for moral reasoning', *Nursing Philosophy*, 2: 131–142.

Janoff-Bulman, R. (1989) 'Assumptive worlds and the stress of traumatic events: applications of the schema construct', *Social Cognition*, 7: 113–136.

Jardine, L. and Silverthorne, M. (eds) (2000) *Francis Bacon: The New Organon*. Cambridge: Cambridge University Press.

Jarrold, K. (1996) in R. Hadley and R. Clough, *Care in Chaos*. London: Cassel.

Jochelson, K. (2005) *Nanny or Steward? The Role of Government in Public Health*. London: King's Fund Publications.

Jones, C. B. (1996) 'Women of the future: alternative scenarios', *The Futurist*, 30 (3): 34–38.

Jones, L. and Sidell, M. (1997) *The Challenge of Promoting health: Exploration and Action*. Basingstoke: Macmillan Press Ltd.

Jordan, B. (1997) 'Authoritative knowledge and its construction' in R. Davis-Floyd and C. Sargent, *Childbirth and Authoritative knowledge: Cross Cultural Perspectives*. Berkeley, CA: University of California Press.

Kamikaze, I., Gibney, R., Carey, P. and Frances, K. (1995) 'Unity without uniformity: lesbians in Ireland in the 1990's' in G. Griffin (ed.) *Feminist Activism in the 1990s*. London: Taylor & Francis.

Kant, I. (1781) *Critique of Pure Reason*. Online version available at: www.fordham.edu/halsall/mod/kant-cpr.html

Katz, S. N. (2002) 'The pathbraking, fractionalized, uncertain world of knowledge', *Chronicle of Higher Education*, 49 (4): B7–B11.

Kersten, K. (1994) 'How the feminist establishment hurts women', *Christianity Today*, 38 (June 20): 20–25.

King's Fund (2006) *Wanless Social Care Review Report*. London: King's Fund.

Kinser, A. E. (2004) 'Negotiating spaces for/through third-wave feminism', *NWSA Journal*, 16 (3): 124–153.

Klages, M. (1997) *Postmodernism*. www.colarado.edu/English/courses/ENGL2012Klages/pomo.html

Ladyman, J. (2002) *Understanding Philosophy of Science*. London: Routledge.

Lam, A. (2002) 'Alternative societal models of learning in the knowledge economy', *International Social Sciences Journal*, 54 (171): 67–82.

Latter, S. (1998) 'Health promotion in the acute setting' in S. Kendall (ed.) *Health and Empowerment: Research and Practice*. London: Arnold.

Lawler, H. and Wells, C. (1999) 'Fieldwork education as evidence of CPD', *British Journal of Therapy and Rehabilitation*, 6 (3): 150–152.

Lawn, C. (2006) *Gadamer: A Guide for the Perplexed*. London: Continuum International Publishing Group.

Lipsky, M. (1980) *Street Level Bureaucracy: Dilemmas of the Individual in Public Services*. New York: Russell Sage Foundation.

Livneh, H. and Parker, R. M. (2005) 'Psychological adaptation to disability: perspectives from chaos and complexity theory', *Rehabilitation Counselling Bulletin*, 49 (1): 17–28.

Lorenzen, M. (2002) *Chaos Theory and Education*. www.libraryreference.org/chaos.html

Lyotard, J. F. (1984) *The Postmodern Condition: A Report on Knowledge*. Manchester: Manchester University Press.

MacEwan, A. (1999) *Neo-liberalism or Democracy? Economic Strategy, Markets and Alternatives for the 21st Century*. London: Zed Books.

Macklin, R. (2003) 'Applying the four principles', *Journal of Medical Ethics*, 29: 275–280.

Mannion, R. and Small, N. (1999) 'Postmodern health economics', *Health Care Analysis*, 7 (3): 255–272.

Marmot, M. (2005) 'Social determinants of health inequalities', *The Lancet*, 365 (9464): 1099–1104.

Martin, V. (2006) 'Learning to lead', *Nursing Management*, 12 (9): 34–37.

Marx, K. (1846) in K. Marx and F. Engels (1976) *The Communist Manifesto*. Harmondsworth: Penguin.

Maslow, A. H. (1971) *The Farther Reaches of Human Behaviour*. Harmondsworth: Penguin.

McEvoy, P. and Richards, D. (2003) 'Critical realism: a way forward for evaluation research in nursing?' *Journal of Advanced Nursing*, 43 (4): 411–420.

McKendree, J., Small, C., Stenning, K. and Conlon, T. (2002) 'The role of representation in teaching and learning critical thinking', *Educational Review*, 54 (1): 57–67.

Middlehurst, R. and Kennie, T. (1997) 'Leading professionals: towards new concepts of professionalism' in J. Broadbent, M. Dietrich and J. Roberts (eds) *The End of the Professions?* London: Routledge.

Milner, E. and Joyce, P. (2005) *Lessons in Leadership: Meeting the Challenges of Public Services Management.* Abingdon: Routledge.

Mintzberg, H. (1992) *The Strategy Process: Concepts and Contexts.* Harlow: Prentice Hall.

Mintzberg, H. (2000) *The Rise and Fall of Strategic Planning.* Harlow: Prentice Hall.

Mitchell, D. P. (1996) 'Postmodernism, health and illness', *Journal of Advanced Nursing,* 23: 201–205.

More, T. (1516) *Utopia.* Online version available at: http://oregonstate.edu/instruct/ph1302/texts/more/utopia-contents.html

Morrison, M., Harrison, J., Kitson, N. and Wortley, A. (2002) 'Joined-up thinking in theory and practice: the case of healthy schools', *The Curriculum Journal,* 13 (3): 313–337.

National Institute for Clinical Excellence (2004) *Research and Development Strategy.* Available at: www.nice.org.uk/page.aspx?o=295953

New York Feminists (1969) in S. Smith (1994) 'Mistaken identity: or can identity politics liberate the oppressed?' *International Socialist Journal,* 62 (Spring): 3–50.

Nixon, J. (2001) 'Not without heat and dust': the moral bases of the 'new' academic professionalism, *British Journal of Educational Studies,* 49 (2): 173–186.

Oakley, A. (1984) *The Captured Womb: A History of the Medical Care of Pregnant Women.* Oxford: Blackwell.

Oakley, A. (1993) *Essays on Women, Medicine and Health.* Edinburgh: Edinburgh University Press.

Oakley, A. (2000) *Experiments in Knowing: Gender and Method in the Social Sciences.* Cambridge: Polity Press.

Office of Government Commerce (2006). *Description of Third Sector Organisations.* Available at: www.ogc.gov.uk/social_issues_in_purchasing_third_sector_organisations.asp

Olssen, M. and Peters, M. A. (2005) 'Neoliberalism, higher education and the knowledge economy: from the free market to knowledge capitalism', *Journal of Educational Policy,* 20 (3): 313–345.

Organisation for Economic Co-operation and Development (OECD) (1996) *The Knowledge-based Economy.* Paris: OECD.

Paine, T. (1791) *The Rights of Man.* Online version available at: www.infidels.org/library/historical/thomas_paine/

Palmer, T. (1987) 'Gadamer's hermeneutics and social theory', *Critical Review,* (Summer) 91–108.

Parker, R. M., Schaller, J. and Hansmann, S. (2003) 'Catastrophe, chaos and complexity models and psychosocial adjustment to disability', *Rehabilitation Counseling Bulletin,* 46 (4): 234–241.

Patomäki, H. and Wight, C. (2000) 'After post-positivism? The promises of critical realism', *International Studies Quarterly,* 44 (2): 213–237.

Paul, R. (2004) *The State of Critical Thinking Today: The Need for a Substantive Concept of Critical Thinking.* Available at: www.criticalthinking.org/resources/articles/the-state-ct-today.shtml

Paul, R. and Elder, L. (2005) *Learn the Tools the Best Thinkers Use*. Upper Saddle River, NJ: Prentice Hall.

Paul, R. W. and Heaslip, P. (1995) 'Critical thinking and intuitive nursing practice', *Journal of Advanced Nursing*, 22: 40–47.

Peters, T. (1974) 'The nature and role of presupposition: and inquiry into contemporary hermeneutics', *International Philosophical Quarterly*, 14 (1): 209–222.

Plsek, P. and Greenhalgh, P. (2001) 'The challenge of complexity in health care', *British Medical Journal*, 323: 625–628.

Plsek, P. and Wilson, T. (2001) 'Complexity, leadership and management in health care organisations', *British Medical Journal*, 323: 746–749.

Popper, K. (1959) *The Logic of Scientific Discovery*. London: Hutchinson.

Popper, K. R. (1992) *Unended Quest: An Intellectual Autobiography*. London: Routledge.

Powell, W. W. and Snellman, K. (2004) 'The knowledge economy', *Annual Review of Sociology*, 30: 199–220.

Quine, A. (1988) 'Empiricism' in A. Bullock, O. Stalybrass and S. Trombey (eds) *The Fontana Dictionary of Modern Thought*. London: Fontana.

Rachels, J. (1999) *The Elements of Moral Philosophy*. Boston, MA: McGraw-Hill College.

Rambihar, V. S. (2004) 'Miandad's six is a metaphor for chaos and complexity', *British Medical Journal*, 328: 1500.

Rich, A. (1987) in L. Segal, *Is the Future Female? Troubled Thoughts on Contemporary Feminism*. London: Virago Press.

Richardson, D. (1993) *Women, Motherhood and Childrearing*. Basingstoke: Macmillan.

Robertson, P. (1992) in G. Siann (1994) *Gender, Sex and Sexuality: Contemporary Psychological Perspectives*. London: Taylor and Francis.

Robinson, S. (1990) 'Maintaining the independence of the midwifery profession: a continuing struggle' in J. Garcia, R. Kilpatrick, and M. Richards (eds) *The Politics of Maternity Care: Services for Childbearing Women in the Twentieth Century*. Oxford: Clarendon Press.

Rolfe, G. (2001) 'Postmodernism for healthcare workers in 13 easy steps', *Nurse Education Today*, 21: 38–47.

Sackett, D. L., Rosenberg, W. M. C., Muir Gray, J. A., Brian Haynes, R. and Scott Richardson, W. (1996) 'Evidence based medicine: what it is and what it isn't', *British Medical Journal*, 312: 71–72.

Sapsford, R. and Jupp, V. (eds) (1996) *Data Collection and Analysis*. London, Thousand Oaks and New Delhi: Sage Publications.

Sayer, A. (2000) *Realism and Social Science*. London, Thousand Oaks and New Delhi: Sage Publications.

Seedhouse, D. (1997) *Health Promotion: Philosophy, Prejudice and Practice*. Chichester: John Wiley and Sons.

Segal, L. (1994) *Straight Sex: The Politics of Pleasure*. London: Virago Press.

Seidman, S. (1994) *Contested Knowledge–Social Theory in the Postmodern Era*. Oxford: Blackwell Scientific.

Sekulic, D. (2004) 'Civic and ethnic identity: the case of Croatia', *Ethnic and Racial Studies*, 27 (3): 455–483.

Selby, R. (1993) *A Bit about Phrenology*. Available at: www.neurosurgery.org/cybermuseum/pre20th/phren/phrenology.html

Seldon, A. (2006) 'Lessons in Life: Why I'm Teaching Happiness', *The Independent Online*. Published 19 April 2006. Available at: http://education.independent.co.uk/news/article358571.ece

Seymour, B., Kinn, S. and Sutherland, N. (2003) 'Valuing both critical and creative thinking in clinical practice: narrowing the research–practice gap?' *Journal of Advanced Nursing*, 42 (3): 288–296.

Shah, H. and Marks, N. (2004) 'A wellbeing manifesto for a flourishing society', *The Power of Wellbeing 3*. London: New Economics Foundation.

Siann, G. (1994) *Gender, Sex and Sexuality: Contemporary Psychological Perspectives*. London: Taylor and Francis.

Smith, A. (1776) *An Inquiry into the Nature and Causes of the Wealth of Nations*. Online version available at: www.adamsmith.org/smith/won/won-index.html

Smith, S. (1994) 'Mistaken identity: or can identity politics liberate the oppressed?' *International Socialist Journal*, 62 (Spring): 3–50.

Snyder, M. (1993) 'Critical thinking: a foundation for consumer-focused care', *Journal of Continuing Education in Nursing*, 24 (5): 206–210.

Society for Health Education and Promotion Specialists (SHEPS) (2006) *Practice, Principles and Philosophy*. Available at: www.hj-web.co.uk/sheps/vision.htm

Stangor, C. (ed.) (2003) *Stereotypes and Prejudice: Essential Readings*. Philadelphia and Hove, East Sussex: Psychology Press.

Stein, J. (1997) *Empowerment and Women's Health: Theory, Methods and Practice*. London: Zed Books.

Stevenson, C. and Beech, I. (2001) 'Paradigms lost, paradigms regained: defending nursing against a single reading of postmodernism', *Nursing Philosophy*, 2 (2): 143–150.

Stewart, I. (1997) *Does God Play Dice? The Mathematics of Chaos*. Harmondsworth: Penguin.

Stewart, S. (1998) 'The place of portfolios within continuing professional development', *British Journal of Therapy and Rehabilitation*, March (5): 5.

Taylor, A. (2003) 'What's new about "the new femininity"?' *Feminism, Femininity and the Discourse of the New Decade*, 29 (2): 182–198.

Taylor, I. (1997) *Developing Learning in Professional Education: Partnerships for Practice*. Buckingham: Society for Research into Higher Education and the Open University.

Thompson, I. E., Melia, K. M. and Boyd, K. M. (2000) *Nursing Ethics* (4th edition). Edinburgh: Churchill Livingstone.

Thomson, A. (1999) *Critical Reasoning in Ethics: A Practical Introduction*. London: Routledge.

Thornton, J. G. (2001) *Birth Counts: Statistics of Pregnancy and Childbirth*. London: HMSO.

Trichopoulos, D. (1996) 'The future of epidemiology', *British Medical Journal*, 313: 436–437.

Tscudin, V. (2003) *Ethics in Nursing: The Caring Relationship* (3rd edition). Edinburgh: Butterworth Heinemann.

Ussher, J. (ed.) (2000) *Women's Health: Contemporary International Perspectives*. Oxford: Blackwell.

von Wright, G. (1971) Explanation *and Understanding*. London: Routledge and Kegan Paul.

Wai-Chung Yeung, H. (1997) 'Critical realism and realist research in human geography: a method or a philosophy in search of a method?' *Progress in Human Geography*, 21 (1): 51–74.

Warren, K., Franklin, C. and Streeter, C. L. (1998) 'New directions in systems theory: chaos and complexity', *Social Work*, 43 (4): 357–372.

Whelehan, I. (1995) *Modern Feminist Thought: From the Second Wave to 'Post-Feminism*. Edinburgh: Edinburgh University Press.

White, J. E. (2000) *Contemporary Moral Problems* (6th edition). Belmont, CA: Wadsworth Publishing Company.

Wight, C. (1999) 'Metacampbell: the epistemological problems of perspectivism', *Review of International Studies*, 25: 311–316.

Wilkinson, R. G. (1996) *Unhealthy Society: The Afflictions of Inequality*. London: Routledge.

Wilkinson, R. G. and Marmot, M. (eds) (2005) *Social Determinants of Health*. Oxford: Oxford University Press.

Wilson, B. (1989) *About Interpretation: From Plato to Dilthey – a Hermeneutic Anthology*. New York: Lang.

Wilson, T. and Holt, T. (2001) 'Complexity and clinical care', *British Medical Journal*, 323: 685–688.

Wolf, N. (1990) *The Beauty Myth*. London: Chatto & Windus.

World Health Organisation (WHO) (1946) *World Health Organisation Constitution: Basic Documents*. New York: WHO.

World Health Organisation (WHO) (1986) *Ottawa Charter for Health Promotion*. Geneva: WHO.

INDEX